RECIPES
for an
ACHING HEART

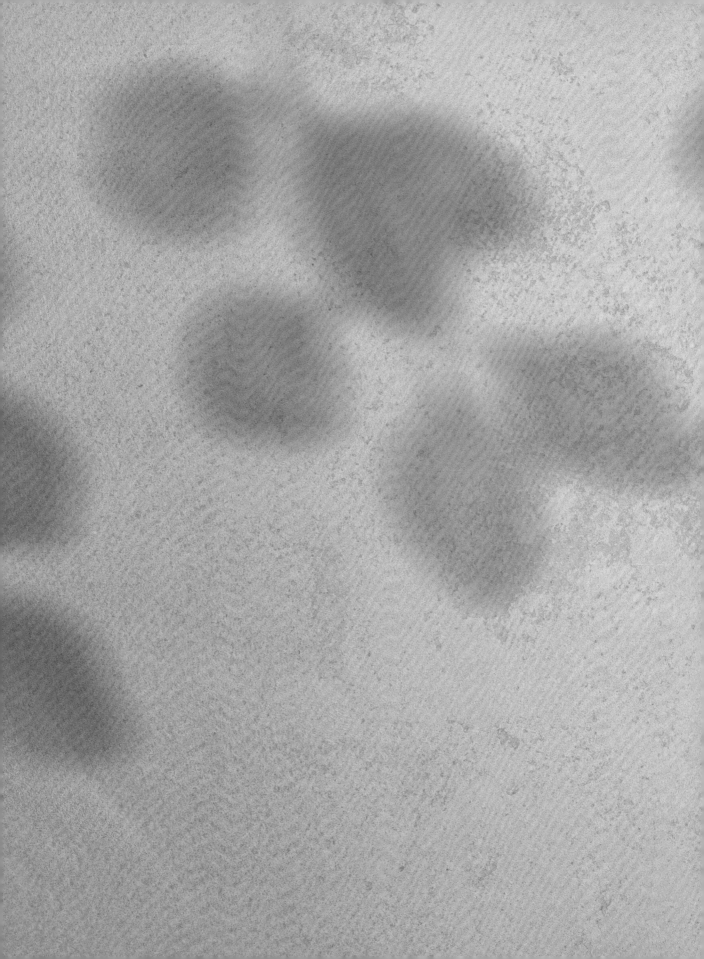

RECIPES
for an
ACHING HEART

healthy & easy meals to help you heal from

grief, loss, or the stress of everyday life

BLUE
HILLS
PRESS

Publisher & Editor: Matthew Teague
Design: Lindsay Hess
Assistant Publisher: Josh Nava
Photography: Laura Lea
Additional Photography: Chelsea J. O'Leary (front cover and page 243)
Copy Editor: Lelan Dunavant Davidson
Index: Jay Kreider

leaf shadow overlay images copyright PhotoSpirit via Creative Market (pages 2-3, 12-13, 26-27, 70-71, 86-87, 106-107, 128-129, 148-149, 166-167, 192-193, 214-215)
wall texture images copyright CCPreset via Creative Market (cover and pages 2-3, 12-13, 26-27, 70-71, 86-87, 106-107, 128-129, 148-149, 166-167, 192-193, 214-215)

Blue Hills Press
P.O. Box 239
Whites Creek, TN 37189

paperback: 978-1-951217-46-4
hardback: 978-1-951217-47-1
eBook ISBN: 978-1-951217-48-8
Library of Congress Control Number: 2023930573
Printed in China
10 9 8 7 6 5 4 3 2 1

Note: The following list contains names used in *Recipes for an Aching Heart* that may be registered with the United States Copyright Office: Airbnb, Alcoholics Anonymous, Bear Naked Granola, BetterHelp, Bob's Red Mill, Chick-fil-A, Cool Whip, Frank's, Happy Tummy Tea, Instant Pot, Nutella, Philips Avance XL Air Fryer, Red Robin, *Silver Palate Cookbook*, Snickers, So Delicious, Starbucks, Sriracha, Suja, Talkspace, Worcestershire

To learn more about Blue Hills Press books, or to find a retailer near you, email info@bluehillspress.com or visit us at www.bluehillspress.com.

Recipes for an Aching Heart is dedicated to anyone who has shown up in their darkest moments—shown up for their children, their family members, their friends and most importantly, themselves. To anyone who has risen from bed to move through another day, even if it took a few starts (or a few months), carrying that lump of swallowed love, that twisted cramp of longing. Your grief matters to the degree of the pain you feel, no matter the circumstances of your heartache. I see you and I honor your reality. And when you cannot hold a brighter vision for your future, I am holding it for you, steadily and for as long as you need.

CONTENTS

RECIPE DIRECTORY

FOREWORD

When Laura Lea first presented me with the concept of writing *Recipes for an Aching Heart*, my whole body lit up with a resounding YES!

My first thought was, *"This is exactly what I needed!"* when I was moving through my very own rock-bottom heartbreak.

And my second thought was, *"How has no one ever thought of this before?!"*

Heartbreak is a universal lesson for so many people, but that truth didn't ease the excruciating emotional pain I found myself experiencing in 2011. I searched tirelessly for books and experts to show me how to heal, and I was amazed by how little I found on the subject.

Despite being a yoga teacher at the time who preached the importance of nourishing and unifying the mind, body, and spirit, my pain manifested into a suppressed appetite and a complete disconnection from my body. My weight dropped significantly, and I was pretty much unphased by the clumps of hair that would come out in the shower, because it took everything in me just to make it into the shower and hold myself up...

I remember WANTING an appetite. WANTING to nourish myself.

One evening, my dad had prepped a lovely meal, but minutes prior to him serving it, I discovered that my ex had in fact been with another woman while he and I were together. It was something I had always been suspicious of.

My stomach churned as I came up to the dinner table. Reverting back to the role of being his baby girl, I burst into tears. I promised him that I was not trying to starve myself and begged him to be OK with me not eating yet another meal.

My dad, who's the opposite of an alarmist, looked at me straight and said, "My concern is that you *are* starving yourself."

I couldn't tell you if he or my agent (I was an actress at the time, too) was my wake-up call. My agent said casting directors were expressing concern and wouldn't see me for auditions until I got better.

Or if it took finally stepping on the scale to see the shockingly low number everyone else was seeing....

But what I for sure remember is that I, like Laura Lea, was committed to searching for solutions to my pain.

I wanted to be healthy again.

And happy.

What I didn't know back then, and that Laura Lea explains beautifully in this book, was how big a role food can play in our healing journey.

There I was—a regular loiterer in the self-help section of Barnes & Noble in Union Square,

(I had never met Laura Lea, and certainly did not know that she was searching for answers to her own healing quest in NYC bookstores at the exact same time!) looking for a solution to cure my heartbreak, and claiming I'd do ANYTHING to get over this person and heal my relationship with myself. All the while, I had NO IDEA that my resistance to nourishing my body with proper nutrients and fuel was only making me feel WORSE and perpetuating my heartbreak.

I was meditating, practicing yoga, seeking all kinds of spiritual teachers, healers, therapists, and even psychics to throw me some gems of wisdom that would provide any kind of relief in my heart. Yet it never even occurred to me that improving my relationship with the right food and developing an appreciation for all the healing and nourishment it provides wouldn't just heal my body but my mind and soul, too.

I know my desperate and devastated self would have jumped on this cookbook in 2011. Laura Lea's recipes were designed to heal us from the inside and out, because she developed them from a place when she, too, was heartbroken.

At the time, I had wrongly believed I was the only person in the world experiencing heartbreak. If you find yourself in that same boat, reading Laura Lea's vulnerable story of navigating her heartbreaks will have you feeling so seen and so NOT alone. Her inviting and non-judgmental approach to acquaint you with food as an aid to your heart will offer you a sense of hope and possibility that I would have given anything for at a time when it seemed like this daunting pain would never go away.

It has been a privilege to coach Laura Lea on her heart over the last year and a half and an absolute joy to call her my friend. You, too, will feel as though she is your most-wise-yet-relatable and kind-hearted personal bestie navigating you through this very difficult time.

As bizarre as it is to say, "enjoy" healing and nourishing your broken heart, and perhaps exhausted and stuck body, *Recipes for an Aching Heart* just might have you feeling grateful for this gut-wrenching experience that led you to a deeper connection to yourself. And that newfound connection may not have been possible without this heartbreak happening for you—not to you.

So, please...Enjoy. In the day-to-day moments of dread when it all feels too much, I couldn't think of a more perfect and inviting way to take care of yourself.

—Claire Byrne,
aka The Heartbreak Coach

INTRODUCTION

———

HOW TO MEND AN ACHING HEART

When this book comes out, I will have owned my business for almost a decade. A decade of creating, testing and photographing recipes. A decade of sharing food in countless forms—through in-person and virtual classes, catering, private chef-fing, writing books and ebooks and of course, in the privacy of my home for my loved ones.

And interestingly, it is in that last space, where this particular book comes in.

You see, for the first 8 years of my business, I actively sought to maintain the shine and polish of my work and my food, despite what was happening in my inner world. I fought to keep them separate, to keep a smile on my face no matter how much my heart was hurting. Even after my divorce in 2018, I took about three weeks off of social media to grieve, and then I dove back into a curated life. I was determined not to let my personal life get in the way of my ambition.

Instead, I overcompensated and convinced myself that I was completely fine, sure that any emotions could just be channeled into work. I thought I had it all figured out as I immersed myself in the process of writing my second cookbook. I would be seen as a consummate professional, a shining example of overcoming a hard season and coming out on top.

I did such a great job at this charade that I actually believed it myself. I believed that I had healed the wounds from my divorce. And I mistook my own coping techniques as a sign that I was ready for another relationship...and then another. I lived the experience of the definition of insanity, doing the same thing over and over, but expecting a different result.

Finally, in February 2021, after a uniquely painful split, I had two critical revelations. 1) I realized that I had absolutely no idea how to healthily process a breakup, and that I had been going about it in all the wrong ways. 2) I realized that I could no longer keep my work separate from my internal healing process.

So I flipped the script, and I started to use my knowledge of food and wellness to create a structure for how I would move through heartbreak.

The first step was to stop treating it like an actual *broken* heart. I didn't see this distinction at the time, but now, as I look back at the last year and a half, I can see that I made a choice to STOP seeing myself—any part of me—as completely broken.

Of course, I understand why we use the word 'heartbreak'. It is the easiest way to signal the

> I FLIPPED THE SCRIPT, AND I STARTED TO USE MY KNOWLEDGE OF FOOD AND WELLNESS TO CREATE A STRUCTURE FOR HOW I WOULD MOVE THROUGH HEARTBREAK.

experience we're referring to, and I will continue to utilize 'heartbreak' below for this reason. But when it comes to the mindset that I need for myself and what I want for you, I prefer to think of it as an aching heart. A heart that is tender and inflamed, but completely capable of repair.

With this subconscious mindset, I created a process of healthy detachment from former relationships and healthy reattachment to self, which I call my Anti-Inflamed Heart Protocol.

When we are freshly aching from a romantic separation or other form of loss, everything feels more difficult and overwhelming. Getting out of bed can be a monumental task. We feel lost, powerless and desperate for anything we can DO to begin to feel better and more like ourselves.

It is so important to allow ourselves to grieve and feel and express a full spectrum of emotions. But it is just as important to have a *system* for healing, because it eliminates the draining aspect of choice and overwhelm. We can be child-like when we're in serious heartbreak, grasping at whatever feels easiest to numb and escape the pain. Creating some loving self-discipline actually gives us more freedom to heal properly.

I believe that the structure I created around recovering from heartbreak can help you in the way it has helped me. And I have had to refer back to it during other difficult seasons, such as bouts of insomnia and intense anxiety. However, please remember that these are simply the tools that work for ME, and you should hold them loosely/adjust according to your own needs.

OK, so firstly I am going to share the general principles and themes that I centered my healing around, which provide an overall healing framework. Then I will share some of the routines and practices that I implement each day.

THE FRAMEWORK

GET SOME PROS IN THE RING

First and foremost, when you are really in the thick of it, make sure you have a professional you can talk to. Right away, book yourself a few sessions with a therapist or licensed counselor, or ask people you trust for recommendations. I have an incredible therapist who I immediately turn to, when I am freshly out of a breakup. I connect with my therapist and work with her initially on regulating my nervous system and getting out of the most acute pain. I also continue to see her to work through some of the *why* behind how I show up in the world, based on my childhood experiences. So, before you take another step, if you feel the need for professional therapeutic support, set up some sessions. I know that therapy can be expensive, but there are lots of ways to get the help you need through insurance OR programs like BetterHelp or Talkspace.

In addition to or after therapy, I would also highly consider the world of coaching, when you feel ready to move into a new way of being as an adult that is present and future oriented.

Most people understand that in order to learn a new language or instrument, we must practice. And mess up and practice again, a thousand times over until eventually, we are proficient. But I have found that people don't apply this concept to cooking OR relationships. We're either 'good' cooks or 'bad' cooks, 'good' at relationships or 'bad' at relationships. The reality is, we can improve *any* area of our lives with dedication, consistency and the right guidance.

I watched one of my best friends transform her life in multiple ways during 2020, and she had been working with a woman named Claire, a.k.a.

Claire The Heartbreak Coach. I devoured Claire's podcast, *Stop Wanting Him Back and Find Someone Better*, for over a year, but I finally reached out after my most painful breakup. And I signed up for her budding group coaching program, which has the same title as her podcast above.

Claire helped me build and sustain a practice of learning who I am and falling in love with ME. When I feel my natural urge to "chameleon" my way through conflict or discomfort, I can often find the clarity and confidence to speak up instead of giving into the urge to blend in. I've seen beautiful growth and improvement in my romantic relationships, friendships and even in my finances, through our coaching. My work with Claire was part of my inspiration in creating my consulting business, where I help women relieve the psychological & physiological symptoms of heartache, holistically. Below is a sample of some of the tools I use with my clients. If you are experiencing heartache yourself, I would be honored to connect with you.

BACK TO BASICS

The next aspect of my healing framework is to make two very important lists. These have helped me enormously in staying calm, grounded and organized when my inner world is chaos. The first list is of all the things that HAVE to be done each and every day for me to function as a responsible adult and keep up with my life. Examples are 1) Taking care of children and pets 2) Showering/basic hygiene 3) taking medications 4) Eating and hydrating (a.k.a. this cookbook!)

The second list is of all of the things that CAN wait, but which need to be accomplished within a week or two. Some examples are 1) Refilling food or household items that are running low 2) Attending appointments or canceling in advance

THE REALITY IS, WE CAN IMPROVE ANY AREA OF OUR LIVES WITH DEDICATION, CONSISTENCY AND THE RIGHT GUIDANCE.

3) Taking out trash/cleaning 5) Checking the mail 6) Folding laundry.

Obviously, these will vary wildly based on your individual life, but the point is to eliminate the chaos of not knowing what to do NEXT and falling behind on important tasks. If you can muster up the energy to fulfill *only* your daily list each day and your weekly/biweekly list a few times per month, you're already doing great. This is one of the simplest and most empowering systems I created, and I still use it to this day when I'm paralyzed with overwhelm.

Another aspect of Back to Basics that I would offer is to do a purging of sorts—an "any season cleaning". I personally remove all items that remind me of an ex (pictures, notes, gifts, even things I purchased for myself but when we were together). But I *also* use this as an opportunity to do a full-home cleanse of anything that's not serving me, Marie Kondo-style. Offering items to Goodwill and coming home to a decluttered space is like a cool, deep belly breath for me. And it's a great space to heal from.

ASK FOR HELP FROM FRIENDS AND FAMILY

Guilt is a feeling that arises from having done something we deem wrong or bad. Shame is a state of being in which we feel like we ARE inherently wrong or bad.

I used to be riddled with shame after breakups. I believed that there was something fundamentally defective in me when it came to relationships. Actually, I should say, I *mostly* believed that I was defective. I was on the brink of fully indoctrinating myself into a story that I was beyond repair. Not only was I ashamed of my dating pattern, I was ashamed of needing my friends and family to pick me up, yet again. And I almost let this keep me from asking for the help I needed.

But I did. Not only did my best friends come to my rescue, as I shared above, my family showed up in spades with unquestioning, unconditional love. I internalize this truth: I can't run far or fast enough away from them that they won't catch up, when bid. I even became so bold as to ask my family members to remind me who I am, quite literally. We created a text chain where they could share memories and offer words of affirmation that helped me remember the child me, the essential goodness and unique qualities of me.

> MY DESIRE FOR HEALING OUTWEIGHED MY RESISTANCE TO DISAPPOINT OR UPSET SOMEONE BY CREATING A BOUNDARY.

I will never, ever forget this simple act of non-judgmental, familial love, and I now understand just how lucky I am to have my particular parents and siblings. If, like me, you have family members that love you dearly but don't know what you need, I highly encourage you to reach out to them and TELL them. Let them make space for you; let them rearrange their days and drive you to appointments so you don't have to be in the car alone and bring you dinner and just sit on the phone with you in the middle of the night. They'll do what they can, and they will WANT to, because you're worth it.

PRACTICE BEING A NO PERSON

While it was clear that going out to bars and partying would not serve me, I chose to be even more specific and intentional in this department. For the first time in a while, I began saying NO to all interactions that I knew would leave me depleted instead of energized. This included phone calls, work projects/collaborations, favors, walks/coffee dates, Instagram DMs, text messages and emails. I evaluated each of these "waves of energy" as they appeared, and I imagined how they would make me feel. If I experienced any anxiety, overwhelm or sense of exhaustion at the thought, I said no.

Easier said than done, right? Like many of you reading, I have a practice of treating 'no' like a four letter word—uncomfortable coming out of my mouth, served with a side of guilt. But my desire for healing outweighed my resistance to disappoint or upset someone by creating a boundary. And my desire to practice being OK with someone's negative response was more important. I knew that all of my relationships, intimate and with friends and family, would continue to suffer if I continued prioritizing being accepted over being ME.

This rule also helped me to realize that I had a few people in my life that I had to "work myself up" to spend time with, people who made me want to take a nap after parting ways. I also said no to people I couldn't be vulnerable with, who I felt like I had to perform for.

On the flipside, this rule emphasized the truly healing people in my life. It was more evident than ever that I had a small group of chosen family, who truly loved me and knew HOW to love me. Friends who understand the ebb and flow of times to serve and times to receive, who have endless patience while also the wherewithal to create their own boundaries as needed. Friends who will sit in the trenches with me, while also pointing out the light at the end of the tunnel. Friends who can say the hard, but right, thing. Friends who MEAN IT when they celebrate my successes, who are never threatened by my rising from the ashes.

INVEST IN REPLACING TOUCH

When I split from a romantic partner, one of the sneakiest sources of pain is missing day-to-day touch. Cuddling on the couch, holding hands, back and arm scratches. Studies on massage therapy show that physical touch can decrease our cortisol ("stress hormone") and increase our serotonin and dopamine ("feel good hormones"). I find it incredibly helpful to combat the abruptness of losing my primary source of touch with setting up massage appointments, reflexology or just pedicures. I know these activities can be pricey, but just having one or two booked for the upcoming month can give you a form of touch intimacy to anticipate. Also, if you're a hugger like me, grab your friends in a big bear hug whenever you see them!

HOLD OFF ON THE BOOZE

I know, it's tempting to drink *more* to escape what you're experiencing. But drinking during heartbreak actually works AGAINST you in several ways. Firstly, it puts off the real work of healing by numbing your true emotions. The only way out is through, my friends. In addition, excessive alcohol can lead to dehydration and electrolyte imbalance, gastrointestinal issues, blood sugar dysregulation, sleep disruptions, headaches and more.

Plus, many of us have experienced how alcohol can lower our inhibitions and lead to choices that don't ultimately serve us. This can show up as sleeping with/going home with someone we meet at a bar, binging on food or reaching out to an ex.

When I am sober, I make better food choices, have more energy, more clarity of mind and often a more positive outlook. It is an absolutely crucial piece of the healing protocol for me. And if you need support in this area, as with every aspect of the healing process, I encourage you to seek the professional help of a licensed therapist or an organization like Alcoholics Anonymous.

TAKE YOUR TIME BEFORE DATING

This one has been the most difficult for me, personally. It's so natural to have a sense of urgency to start socializing and dating immediately. We want to know that there are other cuties out there, other 'fish in the sea' that could be our next person. But as I experienced time and time again, we will NOT attract someone who is right for us from an anxious, lonely, agonized place. If you're invited to events, check in and be honest with yourself about why you're going, should you choose to. Is it to meet someone or to run into an ex? Is it just to ignore what's in your own

IF YOU'RE INVITED TO EVENTS, CHECK IN AND BE HONEST WITH YOURSELF ABOUT WHY YOU'RE GOING, SHOULD YOU CHOOSE TO.

head for a few hours? And don't fall back on the excuse of not wanting to hurt a friend's feelings by turning something down. If they are a loving, compassionate and sympathetic friend, they will understand or at least respect where you are.

If you feel compelled or obligated to show up to a gathering or work event, try to go at the beginning and dip out early. At least for me, this makes it easier to maintain my sleep schedule and avoid saying yes to a cocktail. By the way, if you go the no-drinking route like I did, staying in becomes much more appealing!

MAKE SPACE TO CRY

We cannot escape the moments of deep, inconsolable, crushing grief. But in my experience, the more I make space for those times where I am shaking and sobbing on the floor or punching a pillow, the faster it moves. Some days, I can let it out when the feelings come up. Other days, responsibilities get in the way of a full-on cry fest. But if I get that tight sensation in my chest or lump in my throat and have to push it down, I make a point to sit quietly near the end of the day and gently coax it out. Usually, it just takes a quick trip down memory lane

to open the floodgates. While I don't recommend dwelling on the past, I do occasionally use it as a tool/catalyst for a really cathartic grief session.

CONSIDER AN ADULT ROOMMATE

One of my biggest barriers to relationships ending was fear of being alone. Not *single* alone, but physically alone again in a home. I love living by myself, but I can also quickly grow to love the comfort and familiarity of daily companionship. As my lovely friend Sarajane Case noted in a discussion on this topic, we become attached to someone *knowing we exist* in cohabitation. And I think she's exactly right. I found reassurance in sharing a home, because it was another person constantly acknowledging my existence and finding the intimate details of my life important. If you are in a breakup where you were cohabitating, you might want to consider finding a friend to live with for an agreed-upon period of time. Of course, you'll want to be very discerning about who you choose. Look for someone who is a source of calm, non-codependent support, who you completely trust and who feeds your desire to heal, versus create drama.

TURN TO SOMETHING BIGGER THAN YOURSELF

This part is an invitation without expectation; only you can decipher what's best for you in mind, body and spirit. For me, building a relationship with God (my term, which doesn't have to be yours) and keeping Him/Her/They at the forefront of mind, has been absolutely critical.

Initially, I attended church as a way to connect with my friend Leanne, who I truly feel is one of my guardian angels on earth. But I walked away from the service knowing that I was never alone in even my darkest moments. I knew that I was loved, protected and deeply *seen*, no matter the circumstances of my life. Since then, investing in my spiritual life has been the axis around which my healing spins.

Or, if this doesn't feel like the right direction for you, consider volunteering somewhere. Find some puppies and kitties to socialize at a local shelter, which is always a win-win, or investigate other local opportunities. Before the pandemic, I volunteered at a hospice care center, and it was absolutely impossible for me to think about my own problems when I was visiting patients.

With whatever you feel called to, the goal is for you to recognize your inherent value and how much you have to offer, no matter your life circumstances. To someone, you are precious, essential, and perfect just as you are.

TAKE A SOULBATICAL

From May of 2021 to late October of 2021, I lived in Asheville, North Carolina. I took a Soulbatical, as my dear mentor Alice Randall called it.

While I loved sharing a home with my friend Megan after my most recent split, I also believe that being alone as an adult is one of the most powerful and irreplaceable experiences we can have. So if you do live with someone, considering giving yourself a solo getaway as well. When you're ready, learning to move through the world without the needs, desires and thoughts of another person diluting your own is exhilarating. It will teach you more about who you are, fundamentally, than any yoga membership or self-help book or meditation. When you travel alone, at least in my experience as a woman, your senses become acutely attuned to the world around you. Partially as a protective mechanism, and partly because as women, we tend to show up for everyone but ourselves. We tend to use our ears to listen for a child's cry or a friend's sordid tale or a favor from a family member. We tend to use our mouths to enforce rules to that child or soothe that anxious friend or confirm details with that family member. And we tend to use our eyes to scan our home for areas that require cleaning and the same familiar roads for traffic and our faces and bodies in the mirror for what we deem imperfect.

Perhaps it's just a weekend away for you, in a place that calls to you. Or even a day visiting a nearby town. Read in a coffee shop, peruse antique stores, see a matinee, walk around a lake or greenway, grab ice cream in a cone and sit on a bench and people watch. Or if you're an outdoor junkie like me, research long hikes within a few hours of you. Pack a sandwich, a blanket and maybe even a bathing suit if it's warm enough. Hike until your body calls for water and rest and plop yourself somewhere breathtaking for a few hours.

After my Soulbatical to Asheville, I *truly* began to see my life through a lens of gratitude and abundance, rather than a lens of lack and what-ifs. I now LOVE living alone at 36 as a cat lady. I have more flexibility and freedom than almost anyone I know. I'm thrilled that I rent my apartment, released from the responsibilities of home ownership. I relish the peace and quiet that I sink into at night with my sweet kitty, who is the best companion. I'm able to save money and focus on my current work projects and run to the grocery for a sick momma friend.

THE DAILY ESSENTIALS

Here are some of the daily practices that I follow as much as possible as part of my Anti-Inflamed Heart protocol for repairing an aching heart. Note that, of course, these are tailored for my life specifically. I work from home and only have a kitty to take care of, so you will want to adjust accordingly. Ask yourself where you can find time for the below at your office or during your day as a parent. Get creative and focus on progress over perfection.

1 Practice parasympathetic breathing immediately upon waking: I sit up in bed and inhale slowly and deeply through my nose. I hold for four seconds, then I exhale slowly. I repeat 2 more times (or as many as you like!).

2 Open curtains and make the bed.

3 Sip a large glass of water. I drink around 32 ounces, and I like to add some stevia-sweetened flavor drops or lemon juice.

4 If you have a pet, spend some time intentional cuddling, petting and even chatting with him/her. My cat has been one of my greatest gifts during breakups.

5 Take 20 minutes or so for free-flow journaling or making a gratitude list (whatever writing modality suits you best).I also practice shifting from self-critical to self-compassionate thoughts, which I teach my clients.

6 Spend 10-20 minutes outside, with proper sun protection as you see fit for yourself, ideally in the morning. This could just be sitting on a porch chair, or a leisurely walk.

7 Have some form of gentle exercise *most* days. Walking, yoga and pilates all feel good to me during this time.

8 Shower or at least clean up with basic hygiene and put on something other than pajamas. I also try to shave my legs every few days; it's just a little confidence boost!

9 Loosely work towards three meals per day, each of which contain one source of fat, protein and fiber from a whole foods source. Plus several snacks, usually. See recipe suggestions below based on the stages of healing. But of course, don't put too much pressure on yourself and make space for some treats that sound good to you!

10 Take a look at your MUST list and check off essentials as the day goes on.

11 Tackle work obligations by order of necessity, increasing effort and responsibility as time goes on. I remind myself that self-care is NOT laziness.

12 Connect with a trusted loved one at some point during the day for emotional resonance and support. Sometimes that's asking for words for encouragement, sometimes that's asking to meet in person and receive a hug, sometimes it's to listen about their lives and turn focus away from your own.

13 Prepare for the next day. If it's easier for you and your schedule, lay out clothes for the

following day and do any food prep that will make your morning simpler.

14 Create a luxurious wind-down routine: evenings are always extra painful for me, so I made them something I can look forward to. I start with a candle-lit magnesium-salt bath, and I bring a dessert with me to enjoy. Afterwards, I put on my coziest pajamas, dim the living room lights, cover myself with a faux-fur blanket and cuddle with my kitty while I read or watch Netflix.

15 End the day with a reminder, out loud, that you got through another day, and you can do it again tomorrow.

Finally, before we move onto the food stuff, let me remind you once again: You are NOT broken. Nothing about you is faulty or irreparable. And you are NOT an amalgam of what the world and society tell you about you. You are what YOU tell you about you. You get to define success for yourself. At one point, I thought success meant a two story in the suburbs with a dog and a few kiddos. At another point, I thought success meant becoming the next Food Network Star. Today, with a life that mimics neither of those scenarios, I feel more successful than I ever have. And it's because I sloughed off the cultural expectations for a woman in her thirties. I turned my focus away from anyone else's idea of how my life should be and towards what makes me come alive, what makes a life well lived in *my* book.

You're never stuck. A winding path means that you get to enjoy more scenery along the way.

HOW TO COOK AND EAT FOR AN ACHING HEART*

We've finally reached the part of the story that likely makes the most sense for a cookbook—the food part! While this part is very important, the background is as well. Because this cookbook is specifically curated for those who are in a place of discomfort, of unknowing, a place of overwhelm, a place of lost identity. And because the truth is, ANY recipe can be a recipe for healing heartbreak, if you choose thoughts that serve you. Whenever I teach a class and ask people why they have hesitation about cooking, I hear thoughts such as:

- I hope I don't mess it up!
- This is stressful.
- Maybe I should have just ordered takeout.
- I don't have the time to cook.
- Eating healthily takes so much work.
- I'm a bad cook.

But here's the thing. These aren't facts. They are self-critical beliefs that you are, metaphorically, feeding. You could also feed self-compassionate beliefs, which is what I teach my clients. Self-compassionate beliefs provide unconditional positive self-regard. They feed a desire for self care rather than blame, because they remind us that we are just as valuable and worthy, mistakes and imperfections included. Here are some examples of self-compassionate thoughts:

- It's OK if I burn something or miss an ingredient. I'm learning a new skill, and with every mistake, I become more proficient. Julia Child did it all the time!
- Cooking is relaxing because I use it as an opportunity to politely usher others out of

*DISCLAIMER: The Anti-Inflamed Heart Protocol has not been evaluated by a medical professional, and it is NOT the same as a doctor-prescribed anti-inflammatory diet for a medical condition. Nor is it to be taken as medical advice. Please take this phrase ONLY to represent an overall lifestyle system that helps me heal from breakups!

the kitchen, to listen to my favorite music, to sip a glass of wine or tea or kombucha, to allow my brain to focus on immediate steps, instead of worrying about the big picture.

- Takeout often sounds better in my head than it tastes when it finally arrives. I don't feel great afterwards, I waste food and it's super expensive.

- Constantly having to figure out what I'm going to eat takes up a lot of my time, and it's mentally exhausting. If I devote a few hours each weekend or 30 minutes to an hour each night I can have leftovers available to grab easily. I can cook "Buddha Bowl" style, by prepping different components if I want my meals to feel fresh each time.

- Figuring out why I don't feel great when I'm always eating food someone else cooked takes a lot of work. When I make my own food, I can easily track and adjust ingredients to decipher what the culprit is and avoid it.

- I'm excited that I'm on my way to become a capable home cook, which will make me feel proud and empowered. Cooking for myself and/or my family is totally worth the practice that it takes.

If you actively shift your thoughts in this way, you will be able to use cooking as one healing tool in your arsenal. I had to do this myself, first after my divorce and then after the recent breakup. In my fragile state, I had to switch gears from treating cooking like an obligation to something that could aid in my grief process. I had to ask myself what my job would look like if I could enjoy it and find my food appealing, even in pain.

The result is the recipes that follow, which is why this is different from my previous books (which I still love and am so proud of). Heartbreak is more than a concept; it can have pro-

found physiological effects on our entire body. Breakups have been scientifically proven to have a correlation with depression, and we register the punch of loss in our body. Our hormones can be affected, particularly stress hormones like cortisol and adrenaline, and certainly our appetite and digestion are impacted as well. Most of us have experienced the feeling of a knotted stomach, where very little sounds appealing. Our energy is low, and we feel sluggish from managing the pain and sometimes sleeplessness. There is also research that shows that our emotions, particularly happiness and sadness, impact our immune system.

What we're left with in the thick of heartache is usually little appetite or, on the other hand, cravings for comfort foods that are not health-supportive. In this state, it's natural to reach for the fast-food or takeout meal that will offer a quick hit of serotonin. It's also a time where we may be more likely to revert back to unhealthy eating behaviors and, just as importantly, unhealthy thoughts about our body.

There have been moments right after my breakups where my instinct was to restrict food again. To find false control in making my body smaller, in diminishing myself to, perhaps, diminish my pain. It's a place my brain and body

IF YOU ACTIVELY SHIFT YOUR THOUGHTS IN THIS WAY, YOU WILL BE ABLE TO USE COOKING AS ONE HEALING TOOL IN YOUR ARSENAL.

know, and it can also feel like a quick and easy means of self-punishment. I had the thought "there's something wrong with me, and I deserve to feel empty, deprived, chastised." Limiting food seemed like a quick way to achieve this. In addition, creating physical discomfort felt safer and more manageable than the discomfort of loss. It was a familiar pull, and part of me really wanted to treat myself in accordance with how broken I felt.

For me, the instinct was towards restriction, but for others, it's towards over-eating. Instead of abstaining, they adopt a 'screw it, who cares' attitude. They find solace in fast food and takeout and the cortisol hit that comes alongside processed, sugary and fried foods.

Both limiting and over-indulgence are forms of emotional numbing. And while you should always have compassion for yourself in every season, times of grief or overwhelm is when we NEED to nourish and protect ourselves the most. This is the time to prioritize and bolster our frazzled nervous systems and exhausted bodies. For me, when I felt the desire to restrict, I had to remind myself over and over again that self-love was the ultimate goal, to treat myself as my own

ANY RECIPE CAN BE A RECIPE FOR AN ACHING HEART, IF YOU GO INTO THE EXPERIENCE WITH A MINDSET OF GRACE, PATIENCE, OPEN-MINDEDNESS, SELF-COMPASSION AND RELAXATION.

best friend would. And the path to loving myself the way I want to be loved includes taking care of myself mentally, emotionally and physically.

And I did it with bite-sized choices, pun intended. Instead of worrying about the big picture, I focused on one day at a time and one meal at a time. I left ample room for grace and patience and constantly checked in with my body. I ate ice cream sandwiches in the bathtub, but I also made sure to get a green smoothie or some air-fried veggies in the mix. I adjusted my meals and snacks to honor where I was in real time.

The result was that I moved through the most difficult time of my life more quickly and healthily than I could have imagined. I came out stronger on the other side, and my goal is to help YOU do the same.

So what *does* it mean to feed yourself well during a time of heartbreak or grief?

While the answer will vary with the countless nuances of each body and each situation, this cookbook is an attempt to offer something for almost everyone (grieving or not). While kale salads have a health halo, they might not be the right choice for your digestive system in heartache. Thus, it's so important to check in with your body and choose recipes that sound appealing and which seem palatable for your physiological state. For this book, I focused on creating recipes for all the stages of grief, so there's something for everyone. You might even find some of these recipes to seem so "duh," so simple, that you wonder how they made it in. In my opinion, those are some of the most important ones. Because even with millions of smoothie recipes on the internet and in other books, my goal is to have this be a one-stop food resource for you during your difficult time. I want what you eat to be one less decision you have to make.

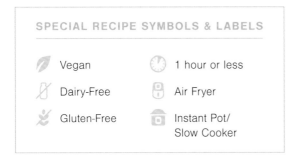

SPECIAL RECIPE SYMBOLS & LABELS

Vegan

Dairy-Free

Gluten-Free

1 hour or less

Air Fryer

Instant Pot/
Slow Cooker

In *Recipes for an Aching Heart,* you will find these dishes have overall fewer ingredients and fewer steps. If they do take longer than an hour, they'll result in plenty of servings so you can take a break for a few days. Conversely, there are plenty of single-serving recipes, which are ideal when you're short on time, cooking for one or don't love leftovers. You'll also see more recipes from the archives of my childhood, which provide so much comfort every time I bring them to life.

What matters more than the content of the recipes, however, is your mindset going into cooking them. Any recipe can be a recipe for an aching heart, if you go into the experience with a mindset of grace, patience, open-mindedness, self-compassion and relaxation. Remember that healing is not linear, and you're exactly where you're supposed to be.

RECIPES IN STAGES OF HEARTACHE GRIEF
The last tool I wanted to offer you, before you dive into this book, are recipe suggestions for that first initial, incredibly tough period post-breakup. This is when even toasting a piece of bread can feel like a chore. And honestly, if all you can do is slather some bread with nut butter, scramble some eggs, or order takeout instead of cooking, I approve! But when you're ready to start making some meals and snacks for yourself, here are the easiest of the easy from my book (in my opinion!):

1 3-Minute Nutella Oats
2 Raspberry Sorbet Bowl
3 High School Yogurt Bowl
4 Best Grilled Cheese
5 5-Ingredient Miso Drop Soup
6 Microwave Birthday Cake Sweet Potato
7 Chick-fil-A Air Fryer Bowl
8 Crispy Broccoli Cheddar Tacos
9 Single-Serving Blueberry Crumble
10 Single-Serving Strawberry Milkshake
11 All beverages!
12 Apple Pie Zoats
13 Strawberry Almond Oat Cookies
14 Rotisserie Chicken Brunswick Stew
15 Southwestern Chicken Salad
16 Instant Pot/slow cooker BBQ Chicken Thighs
17 Sausage, Pepper & Kale Skillet
18 Green Onion Pesto, Ham & Cheese Muffin Melts
19 Quick Tuna & Air-Fried Artichoke Salad
20 20-Minute Shrimp Fried Rice
21 Sweet Potato Tomato Soup
22 Avocado Rice Bowl
23 Cinnamon Butter-Nut Roasted Squash
24 Sweet Chili Roasted Green Beans
25 Air Fryer Worcestershire Parmesan Broccoli
26 Chocolate Blender Mousse
27 Edible Cookie Dough
28 Graham Cracker Sammies
29 4-Ingredient Snickers Bars
30 Canadian Blondies

SINGLE-SERVING RECIPES

———

OPTIONS:

3-MINUTE NUTELLA OATS

Warm, cozy and ideal for a morning sweet tooth, you can have dessert for breakfast in less than 5 minutes! The fiber from oats and healthy fats from hazelnuts will help you stay satiated until you can muster the energy to throw something else together.

MAKES 1 SERVING

½ cup instant oats

¾ cup unsweetened almond milk, plus more as desired

2 drops liquid stevia (sub 1 teaspoon granulated sugar or coconut sugar)

2 tablespoons semi-sweet chocolate chips

Tiny pinch salt

3 tablespoons roasted hazelnuts, whole or roughly chopped

TIP: Use leftover hazelnuts to make my Homemade Nutella Recipe (page 61). Or make a simple trail mix with roasted hazelnuts (10 minutes at 350 then toss with a bit of avocado oil and salt), dried cranberries and chocolate chips (add once nuts are cool).

1   Combine oats and milk in a microwave-safe bowl. Make sure the bowl is big enough to handle the oats expanding quite a bit. Microwave on high for 2 ½ minutes, stirring every 45 seconds or so, until fluffy and liquid is absorbed. Watch to make sure oatmeal doesn't bubble over the sides (just stop it and stir).

2   Add stevia, chocolate chips and salt and stir until chocolate is fully melted. If you like a thinner consistency, add more almond milk to taste.

3   Top with chopped hazelnuts and enjoy immediately.

RASPBERRY SORBET BOWL

I made this every single morning for weeks during a particularly tough bout of heartache. It is so soothing, with a similar consistency to froyo that offered a peaceful moment where I could find few others.

MAKES 1 SERVING

1 cup plain, full-fat Greek yogurt (I like FAGE Total 5%)

¾ cup frozen raspberries

1 tablespoon honey (I love Savannah Bee Company Acacia)

1 Combine all ingredients in a bowl. Using a metal spoon, stir and mash together until the raspberries have mostly broken down and the mixture is bright pink. Enjoy immediately!

OPTION:

HIGH SCHOOL YOGURT BOWL

MAKES 1 SERVING

This was my go-to breakfast during my junior year of high school, when I was too busy and stressed with schoolwork and extracurriculars to wait for something to cook. The key is using grapes instead of the traditional berries or bananas. You can enjoy this bowl immediately, or take it to go and allow the oats to soften a bit.

1 cup plain, full-fat Greek yogurt

⅛ teaspoon almond extract

Pinch cinnamon

1 tablespoon honey or maple syrup

¾ cup 'loose' granola (the kind where all of the oats are separate, not in clusters. I like Bear Naked Vanilla Almond)

1 cup crunchy red grapes, sliced in half

1 In a bowl, stir together yogurt, almond extract, cinnamon and honey or maple syrup. Fold in granola and grapes. Allow to sit for 2 minutes, then enjoy!

OPTIONS:

APPLE PIE ZOATS

MAKES 1 SERVING

This breakfast has all of the warm, spicy goodness you want on an Autumn morning, and it has that extra dose of fiber from the miraculous zucchini! You can replace the zucchini with ½ cup cauliflower, or just omit it all together. If you do, the cook time might be a minute or so less. Oatmeal is always and forever a go-to comfort breakfast for me, and I hope you feel the same way.

½ medium apple, peeled and diced into ¼" pieces

1 teaspoon butter or avocado oil

2 teaspoons coconut sugar or brown sugar, divided

¼ teaspoon cinnamon, divided

½ cup rolled oats

½ cup unsweetened almond milk

½ cup water

½ packed cup zucchini, grated on one of the

smaller holes of a box grater (piece of zucchini approximately 2 ½" long)

¼ teaspoon vanilla extract

Optional: pinch of salt and almond butter or peanut butter for serving

1   In a microwave-safe bowl, combine chopped apple, butter, 1 teaspoon coconut sugar and a pinch of cinnamon. Microwave on high for 1 ½ minutes, then stir to incorporate and set aside.

2   Heat a small saucepan to medium and add oats, almond milk and water. Cook, stirring every minute or so for 4 minutes, or until most of the liquid is absorbed and the oats have a porridge-like consistency.

3   Add grated zucchini, remaining teaspoon of coconut sugar, another pinch of cinnamon and vanilla. Stir constantly for 30 seconds.

4   Serve with sauteed apples on top and salt and/or nut butter, if using. Enjoy immediately.

5   You can double this recipe and reheat leftovers the next day in a saucepan with a splash of water.

OPTIONS:

DUTCH BABY *with* CARAMELIZED PEACHES

OK, so here's the deal: this Dutch baby pancake itself only requires three ingredients. The rest is really whatever you want to add to it. I love this Caramelized Peach version, but I have enjoyed it with many variations (some suggestions below!). However you customize your Dutch baby, it will make you feel fancy and brunch-y, even on your toughest days.

MAKES 1 SERVING

1 ½ cups fresh or frozen sliced peaches (approximately 1 medium fresh peach that is ripe but still has some firmness)

1 tablespoon unsalted butter, divided

1 tablespoon maple syrup

Pinch cinnamon

1 large egg, room temperature

¼ cup unsweetened milk of choice (NOTE: I suggest dairy milk here for a puffier, more classic Dutch baby rise, but non-dairy works as well)

¼ cup all-purpose or gluten-free all-purpose flour

¼ teaspoon vanilla extract

Optional garnish: almond butter, whipped cream, more maple syrup, chopped nuts

1 Preheat oven to 450° F. Heat a 5", oven-safe, ideally nonstick skillet (8" will work as well with the same bake time, but make a thinner pancake) medium and add 2 teaspoons butter. When butter has melted and is lightly bubbling, add peaches. Saute, stirring a few times, until softened and beginning to brown, but not falling apart—this will be 3-4 minutes for fresh, 6-8 minutes for frozen. Add maple syrup and cinnamon and saute another minute, stirring constantly. Add peaches to a heat-proof bowl but don't clean skillet.

2 Whisk egg in a small bowl. Add milk, flour and extract and whisk until creamy.

3 Heat skillet to medium again and add remaining teaspoon butter. When butter has melted, tilt the skillet so it coats the sides. Add batter and place skillet in oven. Bake for 10-12 minutes, or until puffy with golden-brown edges.

4 Serve immediately with peach mixture and any other garnish of choice.

Suggested variations: 1) Scant ¼ teaspoon almond extract instead of vanilla, dollop of raspberry jam and handful of fresh raspberries on top 2) My Homemade Nutella and freshly sliced banana on top 3) Butter and cinnamon sugar on top

BEST GRILLED CHEESE

One of my dearest friends in elementary school in Baltimore was Norris, a white-blonde ball of energy with equally enthusiastic parents. Norris's dad made us this unique grilled cheese combination, and to this day, it transports me back to a time in life when everything felt secure and predictable. Perhaps it can do the same for you.

MAKES 1 SERVING

Sliced or grated cheddar cheese to taste

1 teaspoon Worcestershire sauce

1-2 teaspoons dijon mustard (start with 1 teaspoon and add to taste)

2 slices sourdough or whole grain bread

2 teaspoons unsalted butter, softened

1   Place cheese on one slice of bread. Sprinkle Worcestershire Sauce over cheese; it's OK if a bit runs off :). Spread dijon over other slice of bread. Close sandwich and spread 1 teaspoon butter on outside of one slice.

2   Heat a cast-iron or other nonstick skillet to medium heat. Place sandwich butter-side down, then butter the outside of the other piece. Grill sandwich on both sides until golden-brown then turn down heat to low and cover with a lid until cheese is fully melted. Enjoy immediately.

5-INGREDIENT MISO DROP SOUP

In my experience, high-quality bone broth is healing. Emotionally, physically and mentally. At least, for me. This soup takes almost no time to whip up, and it was truly the epitome of food as holistic nourishment during my breakup. Feel free to cook the chicken yourself; that was just way too much work at the time!

MAKES 1 SERVING

2 cups chicken or beef bone broth

1-2 teaspoons mild, white miso paste (I like Miso Master)

1 teaspoon low-sodium tamari or soy sauce, plus more to taste

1-2 stalks green onions, base and top removed and diced into 1" pieces

1 cup pulled rotisserie chicken or 2 slices organic, uncured deli turkey, sliced into ½" thick ribbons (I like Applegate Farms)

Optional: Pinches of salt and pepper

Optional: dash of hot sauce to taste.

TIP: I recommend pulling your rotisserie chicken while it's still warm, because it's so much easier to pull than when it cools.

1   Heat broth in a saucepan over medium heat until simmering.

2   In a small bowl, add 2 tablespoons hot broth and miso. Stir with a fork until dissolved, then add to the pot.

3   Stir in tamari, green onions and chicken. Cook 1 minute, stirring, then add pinches of salt, pepper and/or hot sauce, if using. Enjoy immediately.

90% of serotonin, our 'feel good' neurotransmitter, is found in the gut/lining of the gastrointestinal tract, the rest is found in the brain. Probiotics in food such as miso, a fermented soybean paste, can boost beneficial bacteria in the gut, thereby protecting serotonin.

AVOCADO, EGG & FETA BOWL

MAKES 1 SERVING

I started making this bowl as a quick and easy lunch that is also low in sugar and high in fat in protein, which helps me feel grounded and calm. While I love the crunch of cucumber with the other creamy ingredients, you could substitute bell pepper, carrots or celery. You can also swap feta for blue cheese or goat cheese, and sometimes I'll mince it more finely and scoop it with potato chips!

1-2 hardboiled eggs, roughly chopped*

1 small or ½ medium ripe avocado, diced

1-2 mini Persian cucumbers or ⅓ hothouse cucumber, diced into ¾" pieces (approximately ¾-1 cup)

3 tablespoons crumbled feta cheese

1 tablespoon olive oil

1 teaspoon lemon juice

Salt and pepper to taste

Optional: fresh herbs for garnish

*My favorite method for hardboiled eggs is 5/5/5: Add eggs to a saucepan and cover with cold water. Ideally, use eggs that aren't super fresh, but of course, not expired. Bring to a boil and boil 5 minutes. Remove from the heat and allow to sit another 5 minutes. Carefully drain hot water and fill the pot with ice water. Wait 5 minutes, then peel!

1 Combine all ingredients in a bowl and gently toss to incorporate. Enjoy immediately!

ASIAN TUNA SALAD BOATS

Another super filling, low-sugar lunch at your service here. This spin on tuna salad includes all of my favorite Asian flavors, and the zucchini boats force me to slowwww down and enjoy a real meal. Don't feel like taking the time to roast zucchini? Make the tuna salad on its own and scoop with crackers!

MAKES 1 SERVING

1 medium zucchini

Pinches salt and pepper

1 teaspoon toasted sesame oil

1 teaspoon mayonnaise (sub tahini)

½ teaspoon maple syrup

¼ teaspoon low-sodium tamari or soy sauce

1 clove garlic, finely minced

¼" piece ginger, freshly grated (sub a pinch of ground ginger)

2 tablespoons kimchi, roughly chopped

2.6 ounces tuna (I buy the single-serving packets but you could also use approximately ½ of a 5 oz can)

Optional: 1 tablespoon finely minced shallot or red onion

Optional garnish: toasted sesame seeds, honey roasted peanuts, cilantro, chives or green onion

1 Preheat oven to 400° F and line a baking sheet with nonstick parchment.

2 Trim the ends of your zucchini and slice in half, lengthwise. Use a metal spoon to scrape out the middle of each half, trying not to cut through the bottom. You can freeze the inside flesh to throw in smoothies!

3 Place zucchini halves flesh-side up and sprinkle with salt and pepper. Roast for 15 minutes.

4 In the meantime, in a small bowl, combine sesame oil, mayo, maple syrup, tamari, garlic, ginger, kimchi and onion/shallot, if using. Whisk together, then fold in tuna.

5 Allow zucchini halves to cool for 5 minutes (this is also delicious chilled), then fill halves with tuna mixture. Add any optional garnish of choice and enjoy!

The initial stages of grief are characterized by elevated levels of dopamine, which is associated with our pleasure/reward mechanism, and decreased serotonin, our 'good mood' hormone. Serotonin is made by the amino acid, tryptophan, which can be in food such as canned tuna, turkey, chicken, oats, cheese, nuts and seeds.

OPTIONS:

MICROWAVE BIRTHDAY CAKE SWEET POTATO

On difficult days, a microwave can be your best friend, and I have yet to see definitive research that it causes health concerns. This quick and easy light meal or snack tastes like cake when you use Japanese/purple sweet potatoes. However, if I'm in a savory mood, I'll use the same technique on a russet/jacket potato and fill it with a little butter, sour cream, salt and pepper.

MAKES 1 SERVING

1 medium Japanese sweet potato (they're purple on the outside with a white flesh inside, sub regular a sweet potato)

2 teaspoons maple syrup

½ tablespoon unsalted, softened/room temperature butter (sub more tahini)

1 ½ tablespoon runny tahini (sub almond butter)

Pinches cinnamon and salt

Optional: sesame seeds for topping

TIP: A "pinch" of salt/seasoning is technically ⅛ teaspoon, if you want to measure!

1 Rinse and dry sweet potato. Prick all over with a fork (just a few pricks on each approximate 'side'). Sprinkle with a pinch of salt.

2 Wrap potato with a damp paper towel (this is key so it doesn't harden around the edges) and place on a plate. Microwave on high for 8 minutes, flipping halfway. If it's not fork-tender at this point, keep microwaving on 30 second intervals until it is. Cool 5 minutes.

3 While sweet potato cools, whisk together maple syrup, butter, tahini, cinnamon and another pinch of salt in a small bowl.

4 Carefully slice slits lengthwise and crosswise ¾ way down, then squeeze the corners together to break it open. Scoop the flesh out into a bowl and mix with your sauce. Stuff filling back into potato skin. Enjoy immediately, noting that it might still be a little hot!

CHICK-FIL-A AIR FRYER BOWL

This was my MOST favorite dinner in the thick of my grief. It offered enough micro AND macronutrients to keep me going until the a.m., and I loved/LOVE the mixture of flavors...especially smothered with Chick-fil-A-style sauce. Is it the healthiest? No. Does it do the trick sometimes when nothing else will? Sure enough!

MAKES 1 SERVING

CHICK-FIL-A SAUCE:

½ cup mayonnaise (I like Duke's)

¼ cup tomato-based BBQ sauce (I like Sweet Baby Ray's)

1 ½ tablespoons dill pickle juice

2 tablespoons honey

1 tablespoon yellow mustard

½ teaspoon Worcestershire sauce

Pinch black pepper

BOWL:

1 ½-2 cups sugar snap peas

¼-⅓ bag frozen sweet potato fries or regular fries (I like Alexia brand)

1-2 chicken apple sausage links, sliced into ¾" pieces (or whatever kind of sausage you like)

Optional: kimchi (I like Simply Kimchi from Whole Foods best, but I'm not super picky)

1 Whisk all Chick-fil-A sauce ingredients together in a bowl or container and refrigerate.

2 Set air fryer to 390° F.

3 Combine veggies, sweet potatoes and sausage pieces in an air fryer, trying to not overlap as much as possible.

4 Cook for 10 minutes, then remove sausage (I suggest using tongs). Spread everything out again and cook another 2-3 minutes, then remove snap peas; you'll hear them popping! Cook for a final 2 minutes and remove sweet potato fries. *NOTE: Times may vary slightly by air fryer model and brand. I have the Philips Avance XL Air Fryer (2.65 lbs/2.5qt).

5 Add everything to a bowl and coat generously with homemade Chick-fil-A Sauce. Add kimchi, if using. Enjoy immediately. Leftover sauce will keep in the fridge up to 10 days.

OPTION:

CREAMY LEMON CARBONARA

You will be so proud of yourself for throwing together this simple restaurant-worthy pasta dish, and it is incredibly satisfying to eat. If you're not into the lemon, feel free to omit the zest and sub lemon juice for whole milk or cream. You can also toss in some steamed broccoli, peas or cooked bacon!

MAKES 1 SERVING

2 ounces spaghetti, fettuccine or bucatini noodles

3 tablespoons finely grated parmesan cheese, plus more for topping

1 large egg

¼-½ teaspoon lemon zest (start with ¼ teaspoon and add to taste)

2 tablespoons lemon juice

1 tablespoon unsalted butter

1 tablespoon olive oil

2 cloves garlic, finely minced

Pinches salt and freshly ground black pepper

1 Cook noodles al dente according to package directions (1-2 minutes less than the recommended time—1 minute less than the lowest number if you're given a range, 2 if not). SAVE ⅓ cup pasta water.

2 In a small bowl, whisk together 2 tablespoons of parmesan, egg, lemon zest and lemon juice.

3 Heat a medium saucepan to medium heat and add butter and olive oil. When butter has melted and is lightly bubbling, add garlic. Stir constantly for 30 seconds-1 minute, until garlic is softened and fragrant, then add salt, pepper and a splash of the pasta water. Whisk, turn off the stove and remove pan from heat. Cool 5 minutes.

4 SLOWLY pour your egg mixture into the pan, whisking nonstop, to form a creamy sauce. You should see small pieces of garlic and zest, but if you see something that looks like egg whites, stop. Microwave your remaining pasta water until boiling, then add tablespoons of boiling pasta water until the sauce looks creamy.

5 Add pan back to burner and turn to low heat. Add pasta and toss to coat with sauce. Add pinches of salt and pepper and more zest to taste. Cook 1-2 minutes to allow flavors to marry and pasta to warm up. Serve immediately with extra parmesan and black pepper, if you like.

The glycemic index (GI) is a value used to measure how much specific foods increase blood sugar levels. The glycemic load (GL) takes GI into consideration, but also the amount of food eaten. Consuming low GI and low GL foods and/or pairing them with protein and fat, as with this recipe, can help prevent a blood sugar roller coaster.

OPTIONS:

CRISPY BROCCOLI CHEDDAR TACOS

This book has a handful of non-recipe 'recipes', which are more about offering an idea rather than steps to follow. One such 'recipe' is these Broccoli Cheddar Tacos, which take less than 15 minutes to make and hit the spot on the dreariest of days. Sub pepperjack and add pickled jalapeños for a Southwestern flair.

MAKES 1 SERVING

2 ½ cups frozen broccoli

Pinches salt, pepper and onion powder

Olive oil

Grated cheddar cheese to taste (or whatever cheese you like)

2 tortillas of choice, around 6"

Sriracha to taste

NOTE: I added some diced red onion for the image. I didn't add that originally, but it's a fantastic complement!

1 Add broccoli to a microwave-safe bowl and microwave on high for 3 minutes, stirring halfway, or until broccoli is fully thawed. Cool until you can handle with your fingers, then squeeze out excess water and roughly chop.

2 Add broccoli back to bowl and add pinches of salt, pepper and onion powder. Drizzle with olive oil.

3 Set oven to broil. Place tortillas on small baking sheet. Split broccoli between each tortilla, then top with a generous amount of cheese.

4 Broil until cheese is bubbly and tortilla edges are brown and crispy (watch carefully, but I like them on the more crispy side). Top with Sriracha and enjoy immediately!

Air Fryer
SALMON & GREEK SALAD

MAKES 1 SERVING

You won't believe how juicy and moist an air fryer can keep your salmon, while still offering some divine crispy edges! I don't keep the skin on, but this is the time to do so, if you're a skin kinda person. The ingredients for your Greek Salad will keep throughout the week, so you might want to buy another few salmon fillets to replicate this dish! I love to serve it with hummus and pita bread on the side.

¼ teaspoon each salt, pepper

¼ teaspoon onion powder

½ teaspoon dried oregano

2 tablespoons olive oil

2 teaspoons dijon mustard

2 teaspoons maple syrup

Juice of 1 lemon

1 4-6 ounce salmon fillet, skin on or off

1 4-ounce bunch romaine hearts, base and any brown leaves removed and sliced into ½" thick ribbons

Scant ¼ cup pitted olives of choice, roughly chopped*

½ - ¾ cup cucumber, chopped however you like* (I like Persian or hothouse cucumbers best)

¼ - ⅓ cup crumbled feta cheese*

Other optional garnish: sun-dried tomatoes, cherry tomatoes, capers, pepperoncini, toasted pine nuts

*Start with the smaller amount, then adjust to your preference!

1 In a small bowl, combine pinches of salt and pepper, oregano, onion powder, olive oil, mustard, maple syrup and lemon juice. Whisk.

2 Pat salmon filet dry with a paper towel, then sprinkle with pinches of salt and pepper, and coat with 1 tablespoon of dressing.

3 Set air fryer to 390° F and add salmon, shaking off any excess dressing. Cook for 7-11 minutes, or to your liking. I like mine on the less-done side, so I usually cook 7-9 minutes, depending on the thickness.

4 While salmon is cooking, add romaine to a large bowl (it looks like a lot but the volume will decrease as we add dressing). Pour another two tablespoons of dressing, then use clean hands to massage it into the romaine. I like my lettuce pretty 'broken down', but you can stop at whatever texture you prefer.

5 Top romaine with olives, cucumber and feta and any other garnishes, then add cooked salmon straight from the air fryer. Add more dressing if you like. Sometimes I can get 2 servings out of mine. Enjoy immediately!

OPTION:

CHICKEN CAESAR WRAP

MAKES 1 SERVING

For some reason, Caesar dressing is a comfort food for me when I am grieving. Later in this book, you'll Asian Caesar Salad as well! But right now, we're focused on the "wrap" experience, with this Americanized little burrito that's full of juicy chicken, fresh parm, crunchy romaine and of course, creamy Caesar dressing. While adding miso paste is optional, I suggest giving it a try for that extra hit of umami!

½ medium chicken breast (approximately 3.5 ounces)

2 tablespoons mayonnaise

2 tablespoons plus 1 teaspoon avocado oil, divided

1 tablespoon lemon juice

Optional: ¼ teaspoon mild/mellow miso paste (recommended if you can find it)

1 small clove garlic, finely minced

¼ teaspoon dijon mustard

2 tablespoons plus 1 teaspoon freshly grated parmesan, divided

Pinches salt, pepper and onion powder

1-2 cups romaine lettuce, sliced into ½" thick ribbons (how much you use is really up to you)

Optional: handful thinly sliced red onion

10" wrap of choice

NOTE: You can freeze leftover chicken, parmesan and wraps, or you can double or quadruple the recipe. If quadrupling, only use 3 cloves garlic.

1. Remove chicken from the fridge and allow it to come to room temperature for 30 minutes.

2. In the meantime, in a small bowl, combine mayonnaise, 2 tablespoons oil, lemon juice, miso, garlic, dijon, 1 teaspoon parmesan and pinches of salt, pepper and onion powder. If using miso, use a fork to smash it against the side of the bowl until it breaks down. Whisk dressing until creamy.

3. When chicken is at room temperature, dice into 1" pieces. Heat a small pan to medium and add remaining teaspoon oil. When oil is shimmering, add diced chicken and pinches of salt and pepper. Cook until golden-brown on the bottom, then flip and repeat until the thickest piece has no pink in the middle.

4. Set chicken aside to cool completely, then roughly chop. Toss with 2 teaspoons Caesar.

5. Assemble: Spread as much of remaining Caesar dressing over wrap as you like, leaving approximately ½" empty around the edges. I use it all, but I like mine saucy! Top with chicken, then romaine, remaining 2 tablespoons parmesan and red onion, if using. Fold into a wrap—I like to fold in the short sides and one long side, then squeeze and roll towards the other long side until wrapped. Enjoy! If you do have any Caesar left, it will keep in the fridge up to 1 week.

6. If you do make multiple, you can store them, sealed, in the fridge up to 48 hours IF using a traditional wheat-based wrap. In my experience, gluten-free wraps get dry and tear quickly.

OPTION:

Of course, pizza has to show up in a cookbook for heartache. Sometimes, I'll have my Personal Pan Pizza for dinner the entire week with a variety of toppings. It's just the right amount to fill me up with some Persian cucumbers dipped in hummus on the side. This recipe is the first in a 'trilogy' of recipes that use the magical combination of thick Greek yogurt plus self-rising flour to create a versatile dough in a jiffy.

PERSONAL PAN PIZZA

MAKES 1 SERVING

Oil spray

½ cup self-rising flour*

⅓-½ cup plain, full-fat greek yogurt

¼ teaspoon each dried basil, oregano and garlic powder

Pinches salt and pepper

Whatever toppings you like! Pictured toppings are pesto, cheddar, Gruyère, red onion and red pepper flakes

¼ cup prepared pesto (I keep leftover pesto in silicone ice cube trays in a resealable bag in the freezer)

⅓ cup grated mozzarella

2 tablespoons grated parmesan

Handful thinly sliced red onion

TIP: Use leftover red onion in my Strawberry, Cucumber & Goat Cheese Salad with Balsamic Vinaigrette, Fiesta Salad Kits with BBQ Ranch, Plantain Nachos with Pineapple Salsa or Charred Gazpacho with Garlic Bread

*Make gluten-free self-rising flour by combining 1 cup GF all-purpose flour (I like Bob's Red Mill best for this), 1 ½ teaspoons baking powder and ¼ teaspoon salt. Sub 1:1 for self-rising flour.

1   Preheat oven to 450° F. Coat an oven-safe 10.25" skillet with oil. Note: you can make this with a 9" skillet if you prefer thicker crust; see below for bake times.

2   In a mixing bowl, combine flour, yogurt and seasonings. Combine until it forms a sticky dough. Add to skillet and spray lightly with oil, then press into an even layer.

3   Add toppings of choice, then place in the oven and bake for 15-18 minutes for a 10.25" pan or 20 minutes for a 9" pan, until the edges are golden-brown and you can get a spatula underneath the crust without sticking.

4   Cool 5 minutes, then slide pizza onto a cutting board or plate and enjoy!

OPTIONS:

1-MINUTE NUTELLA MUG CAKE

This dessert doesn't actually need my encouragement; the name speaks for itself. I will just say; I make my Nutella Mug Cake on those days when nothing, I mean nothing, seems to be going right. When the weather is gloomy and my heart is a little heavy and I feel lonely, I make this mug cake. And it never disappoints. P.S.—Thank you Lelan for the inspiration!

MAKES 1 SERVING

HOMEMADE NUTELLA:

⅓ cup semi-sweet chocolate chips

3 tablespoons avocado oil

1 ½ cups/8 ounces roasted, unsalted hazelnuts (I get mine at Trader Joe's)

¼ cup coconut sugar (sub light brown sugar)

3 tablespoons dutch-processed cocoa powder

MUG CAKE:

2 tablespoons homemade Nutella (sub the real deal if you want!)

2 teaspoons maple syrup

1 tablespoon plus 1 teaspoon all-purpose flour (sub GF all-purpose)

⅛ teaspoon baking soda

1 tablespoon unsweetened almond milk

1 large egg yolk

Vanilla ice cream or whipped cream

TIP: Here are two methods for separating the egg yolk from the egg white:
1) Grab a slotted spoon and place it over a bowl. Crack the egg on top of the spoon, and the whites will slip through into the bowl.
2) Crack the egg in the middle over a bowl, then alternate pouring the yolk into the other shell half, letting the white slip into the bowl.

MAKE HOMEMADE NUTELLA:

1 Combine chocolate chips and oil in a micro-wave-safe bowl. Microwave on high in 20 second increments, stirring in between, until melted. Set aside to cool.

2 Add hazelnuts to a food processor and process for 1 minute. Continue to process while you slowly drizzle chocolate/oil mixture through the top insert. Process 30 seconds, then stop and scrape down the sides. Add coconut sugar and cocoa powder and continue to process for 5 minutes, until completely creamy. Add to a sealable container but leave the lid off.

You can enjoy it immediately, but I prefer to refrigerate it for 30 minutes.

3 Store leftovers in the fridge up to 1 week or frozen for 4 months. Spread will thicken significantly in the fridge. Makes approximately 1 ¼ cups.

MAKE MUG CAKE:

4 Combine all ingredients in a microwave-safe mug that is large enough for it to rise a little. Whisk until incorporated. Microwave on high for 30-40 seconds, until just barely set. Enjoy immediately with a scoop of vanilla ice cream or whipped cream!

OPTIONS:

SINGLE-SERVING BANANAS FOSTER SPLIT

Growing up, my mom would make Bananas Foster as a special occasion dessert, and we were always thrilled to see her pull out the ingredients. But I also adore a classic banana split. So why not have the best of both worlds? This recipe combines melty bananas that have been caramelized by butter and coconut sugar, with the goodness of traditional 'split' toppings. I have been known to enjoy this for breakfast as well!

MAKES 1 SERVING

1 medium-ripe fresh banana (a few brown spots but not mushy)

¼ teaspoon coconut sugar

1 tablespoon cold butter, diced into ¼" cubes (sub cold refined coconut oil; just chop into small pieces)

1 ½ tablespoons semi-sweet chocolate chips

Scoop vanilla ice cream or whipped cream

Maraschino cherries

Additional garnish ideas: chopped nuts, sprinkles, dried coconut, chia seeds

1   Slice off the banana stem, then slice banana in half vertically, leaving skin on. Place on a piece of aluminum foil that can fit inside your air fryer basket. *DO NOT put any aluminum foil underneath the fry basket.

2   Sprinkle banana halves evenly (exposed side up) with coconut sugar. Top with cubed butter and chocolate chips—it's OK if some pieces slide off but try to keep them on top.

3   Set air fryer to 390° F and fry for 10 minutes, or until banana is tender and lightly golden on top. It should be pulling away from the sides of the peel and the chocolate chips should melt when pressed.

4   Use a spatula to gently lift banana halves out of the aluminum foil and onto a plate, making sure to leave any liquid and peel behind (I suggest using a slotted spoon and giving it a nice shake). Top with whipped cream, cherries and any other garnish you like. Enjoy immediately!

OPTION:

SINGLE-SERVING CINNAMON ROLL

Cinnamon rolls are one of my all-time favorite treats, especially when the outside is just a bit crispy but not dry, and the inside is ooey-gooey heaven. This single-serving cinnamon roll is the second of three times that you'll see my 2-Ingredient dough in this book. It allows me (and you!) to create multiple comfort foods without the work of traditional recipes. Need gluten-free? See below for how to create your own GF 2 ingredient dough!

MAKES 1 SERVING

¼ cup self-rising flour, plus more for as needed and for sprinkling*

3 tablespoons plain, full-fat Greek yogurt

¼ teaspoon vanilla extract

Tiny pinch salt

2 teaspoons unsalted butter, softened to room temperature (sub refined coconut oil)

1 teaspoon cinnamon

1 tablespoon granulated monkfruit sweetener or white sugar (increase by 1 teaspoon if not using any frosting)

Optional: frosting of choice (I use Simple Mills Vanilla)

Optional: oil or dairy milk for brushing

*Make gluten-free self-rising flour by combining 1 cup GF all-purpose flour (I like Bob's Red Mill best for this), 1 ½ teaspoons baking powder and ¼ teaspoon salt. Sub 1:1 for self-rising flour.

1 Preheat oven to 350° F and line a small baking dish or baking sheet with nonstick parchment.

2 In a mixing bowl, combine ¼ cup flour, yogurt, extract and salt. Use clean hands to mix into a sticky dough ball.

3 Sprinkle countertop with a thin layer of flour and add dough. Add a sprinkle of flour on top, then roll dough or press dough into an approximate 10"x2" rectangle.

4 In a small bowl, combine butter, cinnamon and sugar and stir to form a paste. Spread over dough. Roll up dough (roll from the short end), then add to baking sheet and gently press down to approximately 2" in height. If using, brush with oil or milk.

5 Bake for 16-18 minutes (16 for extra gooey inside, 18 for some golden-brown edges), then top with frosting, if using, and enjoy immediately (watch the hot insides!).

SINGLE-SERVING BLUEBERRY CRUMBLE

 OPTIONS:

Enjoying a crumble while you crumble...kinda makes sense, right? Seriously, though, warm bubbling fruit with a buttery topping has magical powers, and this recipe is ideal for one-off cravings. This is totally healthy enough to have for breakfast as well.

MAKES 1 SERVING

1 cup frozen blueberries

3 teaspoons/1 tablespoon granulated sweetener, divided (monkfruit sweetener, white sugar, coconut sugar. Add an extra teaspoon to crumble if using coconut sugar)

½ teaspoon cornstarch or arrowroot starch

⅛ teaspoon almond extract (sub vanilla)

3 tablespoons blanched almond flour

3 tablespoons rolled or instant oats

Pinch salt

1 tablespoon unsalted butter, softened (sub refined coconut oil)

Optional garnish: ice cream, vanilla custard, whipped cream, frozen whipped toppings

1 Grab a microwave-safe bowl. Add blueberries and toss with 1 teaspoon sugar, starch and extract.

2 In another bowl, combine remaining tablespoon sugar, almond flour, oats, salt and butter. Stir into a crumble consistency.

3 Add crumble topping to blueberries and microwave on high for 4 minutes. NOTE: for a more traditional crumble consistency, you can also make this in an oven-safe dish at 350° F for 20 minutes. Top with any optional garnish, if using. Cool for 2-3 minutes before enjoying!

OPTIONS:

SINGLE-SERVING STRAWBERRY MILKSHAKE

MAKES 1 SERVING

To round out this chapter and head into beverages, it seemed appropriate to share a milkshake that usually sounds good when much else does not. While I love chocolate and vanilla shakes, strawberry flavor reminds me most of simpler, more innocent times (the strawberry instant Quaker oats, anyone?!). Throw in a handful of frozen cauliflower rice for extra fiber!

1 cup unsweetened almond milk

½ cup frozen cauliflower rice

¾ cup frozen strawberries

⅓ cup freeze-dried strawberries

1 teaspoon maple syrup or honey

¾ packed cup vanilla ice cream (use a full packed cup if using a non-dairy ice cream)

Scant ¼ teaspoon vanilla extract

1 Combine all ingredients in a high-powered blender in the order listed, and blend until thick and creamy. You can add a few splashes of extra almond milk to get it moving, if needed. Enjoy immediately!

BEVERAGES

PEANUT BUTTER BANANA SMOOTHIE

When I'm down and out, little goes down more easily than the classic combo of peanut butter and banana in smoothie form. Bonus: you get lots of nutrition from frozen veggies, and I promise you can't taste it!

MAKES 1 SERVING

1 ¼ cups unsweetened almond milk

1 frozen chopped ripe banana

1 scoop vanilla protein powder of choice

¾ cup frozen chopped zucchini)

1-2 tablespoons unsweetened, unsalted peanut butter (smooth or crunchy!)

1 medjool date, pitted (make sure it's soft and juicy; I like to buy with the pit in to preserve moisture)

¼ teaspoon vanilla extract

1 Combine all ingredients in a high-powered blender, in the order listed, until smooth and creamy. Enjoy immediately.

BERRY GOOD SMOOTHIE BOWL

Cold, creamy and sweet was a winning trifecta for me during my breakup, but sometimes I wanted the satisfaction of chewing my food instead of just slurping! This smoothie bowl covers all the bases, and it reminds me of the days where my painful Spring transitioned to a bright, hopeful Summer.

MAKES 1 SERVING

½ cup canned, full-fat coconut milk

1 cup frozen mixed berries

1 ¼ cups frozen chopped mango

1-2 tablespoons cashew butter (sub almond)

1 tablespoon maple syrup

½ cup granola of choice (I like the Purely Elizabeth grain free Coconut Cashew granola here)

2 tablespoons coconut flakes or shredded coconut

TIP: Want to take this to the next level? Add ½ cup coconut flakes to a nonstick pan on low heat and stir constantly just until it starts to turn golden around the edges. Remove from the heat and keep stirring one minute, then transfer to a heatproof container. Top smoothie bowl with 2 tbsp toasted coconut.

1 Combine coconut, berries, mango and cashew butter in a high-powered blender, in the order listed, and blend until smooth. Use the tamper as needed to get things moving. Patience is key!

2 Add to a bowl and top with maple syrup, granola and coconut. Enjoy immediately.

ORANGE JULIUS

As you've already seen in our Single-Serving section, recipes that remind me of my childhood are often my Recipes for an Aching Heart. I am blessed to have had a very sweet and safe upbringing, which included countless delicious memories. Another such memory is grabbing Orange Juliuses at the mall with my girlfriends in high school. We felt so independent and unshakeable. Whether or not you had a similar experience, this zesty, Vitamin C-packed blended beverage will be a light spot in your day.

MAKES 1 SERVING

1 fresh navel orange

¾ cup frozen cauliflower rice

⅓ cup plain Greek yogurt

1 tablespoon honey

½ cup canned, full-fat coconut milk

¼ teaspoon vanilla extract

1   Make sure your orange is clean. Zest orange, then add zest and peeled orange to a high-powered blender, along with all remaining ingredients, in the order listed. Blend until smooth and creamy. Enjoy immediately.

TURMERIC, LEMON & GINGER SHOTS

When I'm not sleeping well, I tend to catch colds more easily, especially in the winter. Keeping this spicy mixture in my fridge to 'shoot' each morning helps me stay healthy and avoid adding illness to emotional injury. Plus, I find them energizing!

MAKES 8 SERVINGS

Juice from 3 lemons (4 if they're small)

½ teaspoon ground turmeric

Pinch cinnamon

Tiny pinch black pepper

1 tablespoon honey

2 ounces fresh ginger, peeled and diced into ½" pieces

Special equipment: high-powered blender and nut milk bag for straining

1 Combine lemon juice, turmeric, cinnamon, pepper and honey in a glass mason jar (I use a 16 ounce).

2 Bring 1 cup filtered water to a boil (I just use the microwave). Combine water and ginger pieces in a blender. Cover with a dish towel (in addition to the lid), and carefully, slowly blend from the lowest setting up, until it forms a mostly pureed consistency.

3 Add nut milk bag to the top of your mason jar and pour ginger puree into the bag. Being mindful of the heat, squeeze all of the juice out of the bag as you remove it. I compost the remaining ginger fibers.

4 Seal mason jar with a lid and shake until fully combined. Remove lid and refrigerate until fully chilled before putting it back on. You will want to shake the jar well to combine ingredients before taking each shot. I use 2 ounces/¼ cup per shot. Mixture can stay in the fridge up to 5 days.

HOMEMADE SPORTS DRINK

During periods of heartache, I cry a lot AND I forget to drink water, so I'm often dehydrated. This quick, homemade sports drink is a tasty way to replenish electrolytes and look forward to the process. My clients feel the same way, especially as they start to increase the intensity of their workouts.

MAKES 8-9 SERVINGS

3 cups water

32 ounces coconut water

2 cups orange juice

1 cup pomegranate juice

Juice from 2 limes

Pinch salt

1 Combine all ingredients in a large pitcher and refrigerate. Will keep up to 5 days.

OPTIONS:

MOCHA BANANA MILK

MAKES 1 SERVING

The first week I lived in an Airbnb with my roommate Megan, I had absolutely no appetite in the morning. I knew I needed some calories alongside my caffeine, so I started making this Mocha Banana Milk. It took all of 5 minutes to make, and I looked forward to it, despite my sadness. If you're up for it, blend in some chocolate protein powder or almond butter.

1 ripe fresh banana

1-1 ½ cups cold-brew coffee (adjust to taste)

½ cup unsweetened almond milk

¼ cup vanilla creamer (I like Natural Bliss)

1 teaspoon cocoa powder OR 1 tablespoon chocolate syrup (the latter is my preference)

1   Add ice to a large cup. Combine all ingredients in a blender and puree until smooth. Pour over ice. Enjoy immediately.

Stress stimulates the release of the hormone cortisol, which then stimulates the release of blood sugar. Cortisol is primarily directed to the muscles and away from the digestive system, which can cause cramps, diarrhea or appetite loss. Thus when you're stressed, it is a good time to focus on smoothies and soups, like this recipe.

2-INGREDIENT GREEN SMOOTHIE

I love to include a green smoothie iteration in each of my cookbooks. For this book, it felt appropriate to create my quickest, easiest and most simple green smoothie to-date. Just 2 ingredients plus a blender yield a creamy, healing addition to your morning. Feel free to add a scoop of protein powder to amp up the staying quality.

MAKES 1 SERVING

1 ½ cups green juice of choice (I usually grab Suja brand, but almost anything will work)

1 frozen chopped ripe banana

1 Combine both ingredients in a high powered blender and blend until creamy. Enjoy immediately!

HOT CHOCOLATE OR CHOCOLATE MILK

This creamy, rich hot chocolate is a 5-minute method for giving yourself a healthy hit of dopamine. I have been known to mix in a few teaspoons of instant espresso as an extra pick-me-up.

MAKES 1 SERVING

3 tablespoons semi-sweet or dark chocolate chips

1 ¼ cups unsweetened almond milk

1 teaspoon cocoa powder

2 tablespoons half and half

Drops of stevia to taste

1. Combine chocolate chips, almond milk and cocoa powder in a saucepan and turn to medium heat. Bring to a simmer, stirring constantly, until chocolate has fully melted and incorporated.

2. Remove from the heat and stir in half and half. Add drops of stevia to taste if it's not sweet enough. Enjoy immediately as hot chocolate or chill overnight to enjoy as chocolate milk.

3. Optional: Whisk ½ scoop protein powder into the mixture when you add half and half. If it looks clumpy, you can carefully add it to a blender and blend until creamy.

HOMEMADE GINGER ALE

Grief can take a toll on digestion, so I've created a handful of beverages for my consulting clients that they can use to alleviate some discomfort. I love this Homemade Ginger Ale in warmer seasons, and the following tea in colder weather. But you can mix and match!

MAKES 1 SERVING

1" piece fresh ginger root (sub ¼ teaspoon ground ginger)

12 ounces cold, plain seltzer water

2 teaspoons maple syrup or liquid stevia drops to taste (start with 4)

1. Finely grate 1" piece fresh ginger root. You'll want to use a microplane grater. If you don't have one, you can substitute ¼ teaspoon ground ginger. If using ground ginger, combine with 1 tablespoon very hot water and stir to form a paste. Cool to room temperature.

2. Pour 1 can cold plain seltzer in a large glass. Add 4 drops liquid stevia (plus more to taste) and grated or ground ginger paste. Add lots of ice and enjoy immediately.

 OPTION:

MINT GINGER LATTE

I personally deal with an upset tummy when I'm....well, upset. Both ginger and mint can help soothe the nausea and cramping that sometimes accompanies emotional pain, and pairing them in this cozy latte did wonders for me. Feel free to swap out the type of tea bag if your belly is doing OK; Earl Grey is wonderful with the rest of the ingredients.

MAKES 1 SERVING

1 bag mint tea of choice (I love the Happy Tummy Tea by Allegro at Whole Foods)

½" piece fresh ginger, grated (½ tablespoon)

2 teaspoons honey

2 tablespoons half and half or non-dairy milk of choice (the thicker, the better)

1 Place tea bag in a mug. Bring 1 ½ cups water to a boil, then quickly and carefully add to a blender. Add ginger, honey and milk and blend until frothy (make sure to start on the lowest setting and increase from there).

2 Pour over tea bag, steep 1-2 minutes, then enjoy! I keep the tea bag in for the first 10 minutes of sipping.

Are you having self-critical thoughts about yourself in relation to food or cooking these days? Remember to practice shifting to a self-compassionate thought before you dive into the recipe. Offer yourself some kind of warmth and caring: a self-hug, a hot shower, an herbal tea or coffee.

SPECKLED LEMONADE

Inspired by the "Freckled Lemonade" from Red Robin, this is a refreshing, lower-sugar version of their trademark menu favorite. The little bright chunks of strawberry make me happy to see and to enjoy after a long, hot walk. It's also a fantastic mocktail if you're abstaining!

MAKES 6 SERVINGS

3 pounds lemons, juiced (approximately 1 ½ cups juice)

12 drops liquid stevia

16 ounces frozen strawberries, thawed (keep the juices)*

6-8 tablespoons maple syrup (start with 6 and you can whisk in 2 more+ to taste)

6 cups water

*This makes extra strawberry puree. I save it to spoon over yogurt, oatmeal, ice cream or to blend into smoothies. You can also double the lemonade! OR Freeze leftover puree in ice cube trays to throw into water or more lemonade! Lelan also mixed it with greek yogurt and froze into popsicles for her boys.

1 Zest 2 lemons and add zest to a food processor, along with strawberries and stevia. Process until it forms the consistency of a chunky jam, with small pieces of strawberry. Scrape into a bowl or container.*

2 In a pitcher, combine lemon juice, maple syrup and water and whisk to combine.

3 To serve, add 1 ¼ cups lemonade to a glass with a hefty scoop of strawberry mixture and a few ice cubes. Stir briefly and enjoy immediately! Leftovers will keep in the fridge up to 6 days. I personally like to keep the puree and lemonade separate, but you can mix them if you prefer!

BREAKFAST

———

 OPTION: 🌱

I welcome you to the breakfast chapter with these Blueberry Oat Waffles! Making oneself a waffle feels a bit fancy, don't you think? Many waffle recipes require whisking egg whites and extra precise cook times, but these are down-to-earth and forgiving, which is just what I need in heartache. You can also turn them into pancakes; just be sure to use only 2 tablespoons of batter each.

BLUEBERRY OAT WAFFLES

MAKES 2 SERVINGS*

1 ½ cups rolled oats

Pinch cinnamon

Pinch salt

½ teaspoon baking powder

½ cup unsweetened almond milk

1 tablespoon maple syrup

¼ teaspoon vanilla extract (or Blueberry extract, if you happen to have it. So good!)

1 large egg

½ cup frozen blueberries

Oil spray for waffle maker

NOTE: This recipe is made for a classic Belgian-style waffle maker, with dimensions 11.75 x 12.25 x 4. These have also been tested successfully as mini waffles, with the same cook time and no flipping. Otherwise, you may need to adjust servings and cook time for another size.

1 Add oats to a blender and pulse until it forms a flour consistency (it can still have some texture/small bits).

2 Add all remaining ingredients, except blueberries, and blend until creamy. Turn off machine and fold in blueberries (I add them straight to the blender). NOTE: If you don't move quickly, batter will thicken and you'll have to add a few more tablespoons almond milk to make it runny enough for the waffle maker.

3 Heat waffle maker according to manufacturer directions and coat with oil spray. Add half of your batter, spread over grates and cook for 3 ½-4 minutes, flipping halfway if you can. Check to see if you can easily lift waffle with a fork. If not, cook another minute. Gently remove waffle and place on a cooling rack. Repeat with remaining batter.

4 Leftovers (ungarnished) will keep in the fridge up to 3 days or frozen 3 months. Reheat in the oven at 350° F or in a toaster.

Carbohydrate consumption increases serotonin release, so people may have increased cravings for simple carbohydrates during the initial stages of romantic rejection. Focus on complex carbs like the oats in this recipe to get your boost without a crash.

LAZY HOLLANDAISE BREAKFAST

(with roasted potatoes, asparagus and fried eggs)

Normally reserved for cafe brunches, silky and rich hollandaise sauce is now yours with the push of a button! Once you mentally wrap your head around making this 'fancy' sauce in a microwave, you can take your at-home breakfasts to the next level. I think hollandaise, potatoes and asparagus are an absolute dream team, but you could use it as a dip for roasted veggies with dinner, or drizzled on salmon. I also include suggestions for how to make your own Eggs Benedict below!

MAKES 3 SERVINGS

6 large eggs

2 egg yolks, room temperature* (refer to page 61 for how to separate the yolks)

7 tablespoons unsalted butter, divided

1 tablespoon lemon juice

1 pound russet peeled and diced into ¾" pieces (approximately 1 very large or 2 medium potatoes; can sub yukon golds)

2 pounds asparagus, woody stalk trimmed

1 ½ tablespoons avocado oil, divided (plus more for cooking eggs as needed)

¼ teaspoon salt, plus pinches for hollandaise and eggs

¼ teaspoon pepper, plus pinches for hollandaise and eggs

¼ teaspoon onion powder

Optional garnish: fresh herbs, red pepper flakes, flaky sea salt, grated parmesan

*You could easily turn this into an Eggs Benedict meal by toasting and buttering some English muffins, then topping them with cooked ham/bacon/sausage, your fried eggs and Hollandaise!

1   Preheat oven to 415° F.

2   Make Hollandaise: Add 6 tablespoons butter to a microwave-safe dish and microwave on high until mostly melted, approximately 35 seconds. Whisk until fully melted.

3   In a separate small bowl, whisk together egg yolks, lemon juice and pinches of salt and pepper. Slowly pour egg yolk mixture into the butter, whisking nonstop, until incorporated.

4   Add mixture back to the microwave and microwave on high in 15 second intervals, whisking in between, until sauce has thickened significantly, to where it can coat the back of a spoon, 1-2 minutes. If you see the egg curdle/separate, add teaspoons of boiling water at a time, whisking, until silky again. You can go back to microwaving after this. Set aside once finished.

5   Add asparagus and potatoes to a large mixing bowl. Toss with 1 tablespoon avocado oil, ¼ teaspoon each salt and pepper, as well as onion powder.

(continued on next page)

LAZY HOLLANDAISE BREAKFAST (WITH ROASTED POTATOES, ASPARAGUS AND FRIED EGGS)
(continued)

(continued from previous page)

6   Spread potatoes on a baking sheet and roast
    for 20 minutes, then flip and push to one side.
    Add asparagus to the other half, trying not
    to overlap, and roast another 15-20 minutes,
    until potatoes are golden brown .

7   Cook eggs when veggies have approximately
    10 minutes left: Heat a castiron or other non-
    stick skillet to medium and add remaining
    ½ tablespoon avocado oil and remaining
    tablespoon butter. When the butter has
    melted and is bubbling slightly, crack 3 eggs
    into the pan. Sprinkle with salt and pepper,
    then cook according to your yolk preference.

You can either flip them after they've set,
or cover the pan with a lid to seal the yolks.
Place cooked eggs in an oven-safe dish—you
can warm them up in the oven a few minutes
before serving. Cook remaining eggs, adding
more oil as needed.

8   Microwave hollandaise for 15 seconds and
    whisk once more before serving over roasted
    potatoes, asparagus and fried eggs. I do not
    recommend reheating or freezing the veggies
    or eggs. Hollandaise will keep in the fridge
    up to 3 days. Do not freeze.

OPTIONS:

CHOCOLATE CHIP & WALNUT ZUCCHINI MUFFINS

I love sneaking veggies into my breakfasts so much that I wanted to offer a big-batch option that includes zucchini, a la my single-serving Apple Pie Zoats. Healthy muffins are a fail-safe choice when time and effort are limited, and you freeze leftovers or double the recipe. Adding chocolate feels like an absolute must to me, but you could sub with ½ cup dried cranberries or cherries if you prefer.

MAKES 12 MUFFINS

1 cup raw walnuts

½ cup blanched almond flour

1 ¼ cups all-purpose flour (sub gluten-free AP flour)

1 teaspoon cinnamon

1 teaspoon baking soda

1 teaspoon baking powder

¼ teaspoon salt

6 tablespoons unsalted butter, melted and cooled to room temperature (sub avocado oil)

2 large eggs, room temperature

1 teaspoon vanilla extract

¾ cup granulated monkfruit sweetener (sub white or coconut sugar)

1 ½ packed cups grated zucchini (approximately 1 large or 1 ½ medium zucchinis; I don't peel)

1 cup semi-sweet chocolate chunks or chips

TIP: Have leftover walnuts (or any nuts)? For 2 cups (can double): Preheat oven to 350° F and line a baking sheet with nonstick parchment. Add nuts. In a microwave-safe bowl, combine 2 tablespoons unsalted butter, 2 tablespoons honey, 2 tablespoons maple syrup and ¼ teaspoon salt. Microwave until melted, then pour over nuts and toss to coat. Spread evenly on baking sheet. Roast for 16 minutes, flipping halfway. Cool completely before enjoying.

1 Preheat oven to 350° F and line a 12-cup cupcake tin with liners. Make sure oven rack is situated in the middle.

2 Add walnuts to a baking sheet and roast for 10-12 minutes, or until fragrant and slightly darkened in color. Set aside to cool.

3 In a large mixing bowl, combine all-purpose flour, almond flour, cinnamon, baking soda, baking powder and salt.

4 In a separate large bowl, combine melted butter (*I use a microwave-safe bowl to melt my butter and reuse the bowl for these wet

(continued on next page)

CHOCOLATE CHIP & WALNUT ZUCCHINI MUFFINS
(continued)

(continued from previous page)

ingredients), eggs (check for shells!), vanilla and monkfruit. Whisk until creamy, then fold in zucchini.

5   Add wet ingredients to dry and fold until just combined. Don't overmix! Roughly chop walnuts and fold into batter, along with chocolate chunks.

6   Evenly distribute batter between liners—it should come just about to the top of the liner.

7   Bake for 22 minutes, then cool muffins for 15 minutes before removing and placing on a cooling rack. Cool another 20 minutes before enjoying.

8   Once completely cool, leftover muffins will keep at room temperature up to 3 days. Refrigerating will dry them out. Freeze up to 3 months.

STEEL-CUT FREEZER OATS

In my experience, steel cut oats are even more filling than rolled or quick oats, but they take significantly longer to cook. This recipe allows you to prep a hearty, comforting breakfast that you can heat up throughout the week, with all of the flavor already built in. I often can't be bothered to add toppings, but it is wonderful with fresh or dried fruit on top, or with some melty chocolate chips.

MAKES 4 SERVINGS

Special equipment: jumbo muffin tin (you can sub a cupcake-size muffin tin, filling approximately 8 of the oat cups. 2 frozen oat cups will equal a serving)

Oil spray

1 cup steel-cut oats

1 ½ cups unsweetened almond milk

2 tablespoons maple syrup, light brown sugar or coconut sugar

Pinch salt

2 tablespoon unsalted butter, ghee or coconut oil

½ teaspoon cinnamon

1 teaspoon vanilla extract

1 Spray jumbo muffin tin evenly with oil spray.

2 Rinse steel-cut oats in a mesh strainer for 20 seconds.

3 Add oats to a medium saucepan (around 4 quarts) with 2 cups water, almond milk, maple syrup and salt. Stir briefly and bring to a boil—watch carefully to ensure water doesn't boil over.

4 Turn down to a low simmer (small bubbles around the edges). Simmer 20 minutes, stirring every few minutes, until almost all of the liquid is absorbed.

5 Add butter, maple syrup, cinnamon and vanilla. Stir until butter has melted and ingredients are incorporated.

6 Evenly distribute oat mixture between 4 jumbo tins or 8 smaller tins. It should come right to the edge. Cover and freeze overnight.

7 Run a butter knife around the edges to pop out oat cups. To serve, add to a micro-wave-safe bowl and microwave on high for 2 minutes. Mix in a splash or two of water or milk, then microwave again until creamy and warmed through. Add any additional garnish of choice and enjoy.

8 Leftover cups will keep tightly sealed in the freezer up to 3 months.

OPTIONS:

STRAWBERRY ALMOND OAT COOKIES

This is exactly the kind of grab-and-go light breakfast that makes your day easier from the beginning. Make a batch, keep them in the fridge (they're also yummy straight from the freezer), and snag a few before you head out the door. Feel free to sub other berries or chopped apples/pears.

MAKES APPROXIMATELY 10 COOKIES

½ cup unsweetened applesauce

½ cup unsweetened, unsalted almond butter

3 tablespoons honey or maple syrup

½ teaspoon almond extract

⅛ teaspoon baking soda

Pinch sea salt

2 cups quick-cooking oats

1 ½ cups frozen strawberries, thawed, drained and roughly chopped

Optional: ⅓ cup roasted slivered or shaved almonds.

1 Preheat oven to 350° F and line a baking sheet with nonstick parchment paper.

2 In a large mixing bowl, whisk together applesauce, almond butter, honey, almond extract, baking soda and salt until creamy. Fold in oats until fully incorporated, then fold in strawberries.

3 Scoop cookies onto parchment, ¼ cup mixture per cookie, then use damp fingers to form balls, then gently pat to ½" thickness.

Top each with a few almond slices/slivers, if using.

4 Bake for 13 minutes, until mostly firm to touch but still somewhat 'wet'/glossy looking. Cool 10 minutes, then transfer to a cooling rack and cool another 20 minutes before enjoying.

5 Once completely cooled, leftover cookies will keep tightly sealed at room temperature for 3 days, in the fridge for one week or frozen 4-6 months.

Dopamine is a chemical that also acts as a hormone, and it plays a role in motivation, mood, and attention. In the latter stages of grief, dopamine levels decrease or are impaired. Magnesium-rich foods can help support the production of dopamine, such as almonds, apples, avocados, bananas, dark chocolate, oranges, sesame seeds and tomatoes.

ITALIAN EGG CUPS

When I'm having an off day, I love to treat myself to an iced coffee and some sous-vide egg bites from Starbucks. While the cooking method is different for these Italian Egg Cups, the result is similar: a savory, fluffy and portable breakfast that will cheer you up and help balance blood sugar at the same time!

MAKES 11-12 CUPS

Oil spray of choice

6 ounces sliced prosciutto

1 tablespoon avocado oil

½ sweet vidalia onion, diced into ¼" pieces

3 cloves garlic, minced

8 large eggs

½ teaspoon onion powder

1 teaspoon dried oregano

¼-½ teaspoon salt (¼ if using feta, ½ if using goat cheese)

½ teaspoon black pepper

1 teaspoon Worcestershire sauce

½ cup sun-dried tomatoes in olive oil, excess oil shaken off and roughly chopped

2.5 ounces goat cheese or feta cheese, crumbled

1   Preheat oven 375° F. Spray a 12-cup muffin tin with oil spray.

2   Cut prosciutto in half crosswise (I use kitchen shears) and overlap the pieces in each cup, arranging so it covers as much as possible. Fold any edges back into the cup that are hanging over. It's OK if you only get 11 cups.

3   Heat a small skillet to medium and add avocado oil. When oil moves quickly around the pan, add onion. Saute, stirring frequently, until softened and translucent, 3-4 minutes. Add garlic, stirring constantly for 30 seconds, then set aside to cool at least 5 minutes.

4   In a large mixing bowl (ideally with a spout), whisk together eggs, onion powder, oregano, salt, pepper, and Worcestershire. In a separate small bowl, combine sun-dried tomatoes, goat cheese, and onion. Add one tablespoon of the tomato, cheese, and onion mixture to each cup, then evenly distribute any remaining filling. Evenly top with egg mixture.

5   Bake for 20 minutes, until bouncy and firm to touch. Cool 10 minutes before running a butter knife around the edges and removing.

6   Leftover egg cups will keep tightly sealed in the fridge up to 5 days or frozen 2 months. Reheat in the microwave, in a 300° F oven or in the air fryer for 3-4 minutes. If they're frozen, add egg cups to fridge the night before you want to enjoy, then reheat as above.

SAUSAGE, MUSHROOM & SWISS FRITTATA

If you've been in my community for a while, you know I love a frittata. They could really go into the entree section, because they're so incredibly versatile. This mushroom and swiss iteration is my favorite to-date, and it's an easy way to give yourself some extra TLC. Maybe even bring out a cloth napkin and read a chapter of a book over a slice.

MAKES 4-6 SERVINGS

9 large eggs

2 teaspoons balsamic vinegar

½ teaspoon salt

½ teaspoon black pepper

½ teaspoon garlic powder

1 teaspoon dried thyme

¼ cup unsweetened plain almond milk

4 ounces swiss cheese, grated (approximately 1 ½ cups grated)

8 ounces ground breakfast sausage

2 tablespoon unsalted butter

½ medium yellow onion, diced into ¼" pieces

8 ounces pre-sliced baby bella or white button mushrooms, excess dirt removed by gently wiping with a paper towel (sub 1 green bell pepper, diced into ½" pieces, if you're not into mushrooms!)

TIP: Save the other 8 ounces of a 16-ounce package to make breakfast sausage patties for my 3-Ingredient Honey Biscuits.

1 Preheat oven to 375° F.

2 Crack eggs into a mixing bowl. Whisk, then stir in balsamic, salt, pepper, garlic powder, thyme, almond milk and grated cheese.

3 Heat a large cast-iron or other nonstick skillet to medium heat. Add sausage. Cook, breaking up with a spatula, until golden-brown, 6-8 minutes. Scrape into a heatproof bowl, draining any excess grease. Add butter, onion and mushrooms to skillet. Cook, stirring every few minutes for 12 minutes, or until mushrooms have reduced in size and veggies have golden-brown edges.

4 Turn off heat and add cooked sausage and egg mixture, stirring until incorporated. Add skillet to the oven and bake for 18 minutes, until firm to touch on top.

5 Leftover frittata will keep tightly sealed in the fridge up to 5 days. I don't recommend reheating.

 OPTION:

3-INGREDIENT HONEY BISCUITS

This is the last recipe that uses my 2-ingredient dough to create something special with very little effort. I made these Honey Biscuits often when I lived in Asheville. Even though that was a joyful time in my life, having made my way through the thick of grief, there were still some glum moments. A few biscuits with butter on my tiny porch, overlooking the Blue Ridge, never failed to do me good.

MAKES 4 BISCUITS

1 ¼ cups self-rising flour, plus more for dusting

1 tablespoon honey, plus more for topping

¾ cup plain, full-fat Greek yogurt (it must be Greek yogurt for this to work!)

Optional: large egg for an egg wash

Butter and flaky sea salt for topping, or whatever toppings you prefer!

TIP: Make gluten-free self-rising flour by combining 1 cup GF all-purpose flour (I like Bob's Red Mill best for this), 1 ½ teaspoons baking powder and ¼ teaspoon salt. Sub 1:1 for self-rising flour.

1 Preheat oven to 375° F and line a baking sheet with nonstick parchment.

2 In a mixing bowl, combine flour, 1 tablespoon honey and yogurt. Use clean hands to mix until it forms a shaggy dough, then turn it out onto a lightly floured surface.

3 Form into a square roughly 8"x8"x¾" Slice into 4 even-sized pieces, and gently lift them onto baking sheet with a spatula. Leave at least ½" between each. Optional: whisk egg and brush biscuits with egg wash for a golden color.

4 Bake biscuits for 23 minutes, then cool 3 minutes before slicing and adding butter and honey, or whatever you prefer!

5 Leftover biscuits will keep in the fridge up to three days. Reheat in the oven at 400° F, in the air fryer at 390° F, until the edges are crispy again. I also LOVE these biscuits with butter and honey or jam. I don't recommend freezing.

POULTRY ENTRÉES

———

ROTISSERIE CHICKEN BRUNSWICK STEW

My mom's Brunswick Stew was one of my favorite recipes growing up in Baltimore (before we moved to Nashville), so I thought it was the perfect recipe to usher in our entrées. It has just the right balance of acidity, sweetness and heartiness that leaves you wanting more. I don't usually go for brothy soups, but I'll always have a soft spot for Brunswick Stew and the feeling of family and safety that it evokes. P.S. Traditional recipes include other ingredients, such as pork, briset and canned corn, but I simplified...I think with success!

MAKES 6-8 SERVINGS

1 medium rotisserie chicken, meat pulled off (I suggest the plain or salt and pepper flavor. Sub 1 ¾ pound boneless chicken breasts or thighs and cook in an Instant Pot or slow cooker)

3 cloves garlic, minced

16 ounce can butter beans, rinsed and drain

2 tablespoons avocado oil

1 small yellow onion, diced into ¼" pieces

½ teaspoon paprika

½ teaspoon salt

¼ teaspoon pepper

½ cup tomato-based BBQ sauce (can you store-bought or the recipes from my Instant Pot BBQ Chicken Thighs page 123)

3 tablespoons Worcestershire sauce

2 teaspoons dijon mustard

15 ounce can diced tomatoes

15 ounce can tomato sauce

32 ounces chicken broth

12 ounces frozen mixed veggies

1 Heat a large soup or stock pot to medium and add avocado oil. When oil moves quickly around the pan, add diced onion. Saute 3-4 minutes, until softened and translucent. Turn heat to low and add a splash of water, garlic, paprika, salt and pepper. Stir constantly for 30 seconds.

2 Add pulled chicken, BBQ sauce, Worcestershire sauce, dijon mustard, diced tomatoes, tomato sauce, 2 cups water and broth. Stir and bring to a simmer.

3 Simmer soup for 15 minutes, then add frozen mixed veggies and butter beans. Simmer until veggies are thawed and warmed through. Add more seasoning to taste before serving.

4 Reheat on the stove. Leftovers will keep tightly sealed in the fridge up to 4 days or frozen 3 months (you may want to freeze in individual servings).

SWEET & SOUR CHICKEN

I make this sweet and sour chicken often, including in my classes. Who doesn't want to feel like they're enjoying takeout from the couch, and healthier?! I like to enjoy mine with my Perfect Jasmine Rice, Roasted Broccoli and a hefty dollop of kimchi. Also, you can swap the sauce for another that you like, such as Honey Mustard or my Buffalo Aioli; the cooking technique of using the egg wash last before searing is the mainstay!

MAKES 6 SERVINGS

1 ½ pounds boneless, skinless chicken breasts

1 bunch green onions

2 tablespoons avocado oil

¾ teaspoon salt, divided

¾ teaspoon pepper, divided

2 cloves garlic, minced

⅓ cup honey

½ cup vinegar

¼ cup ketchup

2 tablespoons low-sodium tamari or soy sauce

½ cup cornstarch or arrowroot starch

2 eggs

1. Allow chicken to rest at room temperature while you prepare the pre-cooking steps.

2. Preheat oven to 375° F and grease a 13"×11" baking dish.

3. In a bowl, whisk together garlic, honey, vinegar, ketchup and tamari. Set aside.

4. In a large ziplock bag, combine arrowroot or cornstarch, ½ teaspoon each salt and pepper and diced chicken. Seal and shake to coat. Whisk eggs in a shallow bowl.

5. Turn on exhaust fan and grab a heat-proof bowl. Heat a large skillet to medium and add 2 tablespoons avocado oil. When a splash of water sizzles, you're ready.

6. Dip a few chicken pieces in egg, shake off excess, then add to pan. Repeat until pan is full with no overlap, then cook until golden-brown on the bottom. Flip and cook another minute. Chicken doesn't need to be fully cooked in the pan. Place in bowl and repeat with remaining chicken. You can add oil as needed, and you might need to adjust the heat down as you cook.

7. Pour sweet and sour sauce over chicken and add the 1" green onion pieces. Toss to coat. Add chicken to a second baking sheet. Bake for 25 minutes, flipping halfway.

8. Reheat chicken in the oven at 400° F until just warmed through, or in the air fryer for 3-5 minutes at 390° F. Leftovers of all three will keep tightly sealed in the fridge up to 4 days, or in the freezer 2 months.

SOUTHWESTERN CHICKEN SALAD

What we crave during heartache is so subjective, but for me, chicken salad sits near the top of the list. Perhaps because it reminds me of my grandmother, my Noni, who had chicken salad almost every day for lunch. This Southwestern variation is my favorite to make in warmer months, and I love scooping it with tortilla chips.

MAKES 6 SERVINGS

¼ cup lime juice (approximately 3 limes)

½ cup mayonnaise

1 tablespoon honey

1 clove garlic, minced

2 teaspoons chili powder

½ teaspoon cumin

¼ teaspoon salt

¼ teaspoon pepper

1 store-bought rotisserie chicken (look for plain or salt and pepper), shredded

15 ounce can black beans, drained and rinsed

1 medium shallot, minced into ¼" pieces

1 pint cherry tomatoes, sliced in half

2 ears fresh corn, removed from cob

Serve with chopped cilantro, green onions, and tortilla chips

TIP: Turn this into a Waldorf Chicken Salad by subbing lemon juice for lime, 1 teaspoon onion powder for chili powder, garlic powder for cumin, sliced grapes for black beans, 1 cup chopped walnuts for tomatoes and 2 cups sliced celery for corn.

1 In a large mixing bowl, whisk together all sauce ingredients.

2 Fold in black beans, shredded chicken, cherry tomatoes, minced shallot and corn kernels. Mix everything together until evenly incorporated. Taste for more seasoning. Refrigerate 30 minutes before enjoying.

3 Serve with fresh cilantro or green onions and tortilla chips.

4 Leftovers will keep in the fridge up to 4 days. I don't recommend freezing.

OPTION:

Air Fryer
SPICY
CHICKEN
SAMMIES

One of my favorite fast-food items is a spicy chicken sandwich; can I get an amen? It happens rarely, but that crispy chicken goodness hits the tastebuds just right. My body on the other hand? Not pleased. In order to satisfy my palate AND take care of myself, I created this air-fryer version...and I truly prefer it! If you're not into spice: use all pickle juice instead of Frank's, reduce or omit the cayenne and swap Pepper Jack for your cheese of choice.

MAKES 4 SERVINGS

1 ¼ pounds chicken breasts (usually 2 medium sized breasts)

¾ cup (I drain from a 24 ounce jar, and it doesn't affect the pickles staying fresh in the fridge!)

¼ cup Frank's Red Hot original

½ cup all-purpose or GF all-purpose flour

¼ teaspoon each salt and pepper

2 large eggs

¾ cup panko/Japanese-style bread crumbs (sub GF panko breadcrumbs)

1 ½ teaspoons cayenne pepper.

1 teaspoon garlic powder

1 teaspoon onion powder

½ teaspoon paprika

Oil spray

Pepper Jack cheese (enough for four sandwiches)

Buns

Thinly sliced dill pickles

Optional additional garnish: lettuce, tomato, red onion,my Homemade Chick-fil-A Sauce (page 49), mustard, mayo, ketchup

TIP: You might have some leftover breadcrumbs. You can freeze them and they'll last for MONTHS in the freezer.

1 Place chicken between two pieces of parchment paper and use a meat mallet (or a hammer :)) to pound breasts lightly into 1" thickness. If they're already thin, just use the mallet to make sure they're an even thickness. Slice breasts in half crosswise to form 4 cutlets.

2 In a shallow dish or resealable bag, combine pickle juice, Frank's and chicken. Cover or seal and make sure cutlets are fully covered in marinade. Marinate for 2 hours in the fridge, removing 30 minutes before cooking.

3 After 30 minutes at room temp, take cutlets out of marinade and pat thoroughly dry. Place on a plate or baking sheet.

4 Whisk eggs in a shallow bowl. In a separate, larger bowl, combine flour, salt and pepper and whisk to incorporate.

5 Dredge cutlets in flour mixture. Place back on plate.

6 To the flour bowl, add panko, cayenne, garlic powder, onion powder and paprika. Whisk to incorporate.

(continued on next page)

AIR FRYER SPICY CHICKEN SAMMIES
(continued)

(continued from previous page)

7   Dredge cutlets in eggs, then press into panko mixture, making sure to get into all cracks and crevices!

8   Spray air fryer basket with oil. Add 2 cutlets and spray with a light layer of oil. Set air fryer to 390° F and cook for 15 minutes, flipping and spraying bottom approximately halfway, or until crust is golden-brown. Place cooked cutlets on paper towel and repeat with remaining raw cutlets.

9   To assemble, I like to toast the buns in the oven with a slice of Pepper Jack on top. Then add pickles and whatever garnish you prefer. Enjoy immediately!

10 Reheat cutlets in the air fryer for 2-3 minutes, or just until warmed through. They will be a little bit dry the second time around, but still yummy with all of the fixings. Leftovers will keep in the fridge up to 3 days. I don't recommend freezing once cooked, but you could prepare them up to dredging in panko, then place on a parchment lined baking sheet, wrap tightly and freeze up to a week.

Heartache has been likened to withdrawal from an addiction. When we cannot have our beloved ex, we may replace the craving with food cravings. Knowing this can help you have compassion for what you're experiencing. If you've been heading for fast food, a recipe like this can be a healthier replacement to satisfying those cravings.

TURKEY ENCHILADAS *with* ROASTED RED PEPPER SAUCE

OPTION:

These enchiladas take a bit more time than other dishes in the book, but they are so rewarding...even if everything else feels out of control. A hit with adults and littles, this recipe is perfect for a cozy weekend afternoon, and you'll likely have even better leftovers.

MAKES 8 SERVINGS

RED PEPPER SAUCE:

1 cup roasted red peppers

15 ounce can diced tomatoes

1 clove garlic, roughly chopped (can minced the garlic below at the same time)

1 tablespoon chili powder

1 teaspoon onion powder

½ teaspoon cumin

¼ teaspoon salt

1 tablespoon arrowroot starch or cornstarch

ENCHILADA:

8 ounces mild cheddar cheese, grated

1 tablespoon avocado oil

1 pound ground turkey (I suggest a mixture of dark and light meat)

1 small yellow onion, diced into ¼" pieces

Red bell pepper, diced into ¼" pieces

¾ pound russet potatoes, cleaned and diced into ½" pieces (approximately 2 potatoes. And yes, these are small pieces of potato so they can cook evenly!)

2 cloves garlic, minced

½ teaspoon chili powder

¼ teaspoon cumin

½ teaspoon salt

10-12 7-inch tortillas

Optional garnish: avocado, chives, cilantro, sour cream, salsa etc.

1 Make Roasted Red Pepper Enchilada Sauce: Combine all ingredients in a blender and blend until creamy. Pour in a medium saucepan.

2 Bring sauce to a simmer. Mix starch in a small bowl with 2 tablespoons water until combined, then pour into sauce. Cook, stirring, another 2-3 minutes, until noticeably thickened. Set aside.

3 Preheat oven to 350° F and grease a 13"×9"×2" baking dish.

(continued on next page)

TURKEY ENCHILADAS WITH ROASTED RED PEPPER SAUCE

(continued)

(continued from previous page)

4   Heat a large saucepan or pot to medium heat and add tablespoon avocado oil. When oil moves quickly around the pan, add turkey. Cook, breaking up as you go, until golden-brown around the edges and no pink remains. Scrape into a heat-proof bowl.

5   Add ½ cup water to the pot and scrape up browned bits from the bottom, then add diced onions, bell peppers and potatoes. Cook, stirring every few minutes, until potatoes have golden-brown edges, 10 minutes (they'll keep cooking).

6   Turn heat to low and add minced garlic, chili powder, cumin, salt, cooked turkey and ½ cup Enchilada Sauce. Stir to evenly incorporate and simmer 5 minutes. Remove from heat.

7   Fill each tortilla with ½ cup of turkey mixture, then sprinkle with 1 tablespoon grated cheese. Roll up and place seam-side down in baking dish. Repeat until no mixture remains, then cover with enchilada sauce and remaining cheese.

8   Cover with aluminum foil and bake 35 minutes. Uncover and broil, watching closely, until cheese is bubbling and edges are golden-brown. Cool 10 minutes before serving with garnishes of choice.

9   Reheat in the oven at 350° F. Leftover enchiladas will keep in the fridge up to 4 days. If you want to freeze, follow all steps *before* adding Enchilada Sauce on top. Store in freezer separately up to 2 months. When you want to serve, move enchiladas from the freezer to the fridge the night before. Cover with sauce and cheese just before baking, and cook as directed.

SESAME CRUSTED CHICKEN & WILTED SPINACH SALADS

 OPTION:

I grew up visiting my grandparents in Jacksonville, Florida, and it was during one of these trips that I first tried the inspiration for my Sesame Crusted Chicken and Wilted Spinach Salad. I will never forget how the flavors and texture lit up my brain and my tastebuds like a Christmas tree, and I would order the same meal every year until we no longer visited. Whenever I make this salad, I quite literally feel the joy that comes from sitting around a table with my core unit, eating something wonderful.

MAKES 4 SERVINGS

1 ½ pounds boneless, skinless chicken breasts

3 tablespoons toasted sesame oil

½ cup plus 2 tablespoons avocado oil

3 tablespoons tamari or soy sauce

3 tablespoons maple syrup

2 cloves garlic, minced

Lime

½ cup all-purpose flour

⅓ cup sesame seeds

¼ each salt, pepper, garlic powder and onion powder

2 large eggs

10 ounces fresh baby spinach

Optional garnish: avocado, cucumber, honey roasted peanuts or roasted and salted cashew, grilled halloumi cheese

TIP: Rinse skillets while still hot with cold water for easier cleaning.

TIP: Ideas for leftover sesame seeds: as a crust for seared tuna, add to roasted veggies with a drizzle of toasted sesame oil, sprinkled on salads. Store in freezer to extend freshness. Toss cashews with maple syrup, avocado oil and sprinkle sesame seeds and salt on top. Roast until golden brown.

1 Slice chicken breasts in half, crosswise, and place between two pieces of parchment paper. NOTE: if one of the chicken breasts is significantly bigger than the other, cut into 3 pieces, crosswise. Use a mallet to pound all chicken to ¾" thickness. Add to a gallon ziplock bag.

2 In a blender, combine toasted sesame oil, oil, tamari, maple syrup, garlic and juice from your lime. Blend until creamy.

3 Add 3 tablespoons dressing to the chicken. Seal and shake to coat. Set aside at room temperature while you prep the rest. You can also marinate up to overnight in the fridge.

(continued on next page)

SESAME CRUSTED CHICKEN & WILTED SPINACH SALADS

(continued)

(continued from previous page)

4   In a shallow dish, combine flour, sesame seeds, salt, pepper, garlic powder and onion powder.

5   Whisk eggs in another shallow dish.

6   Grab a clean plate. Dip chicken in the egg mixture, then into the flour/sesame mixture, shaking off excess. Place on a baking sheet.

7   Turn on oven exhaust fan. Heat a large cast-iron or other nonstick, oven-safe skillet to medium-high heat and add remaining 2 tablespoons avocado oil. When oil moves quickly around pan, add half of your chicken pieces. Sear for 4-6 minutes, or until the bottoms are golden-brown and you can easily flip without sticking. Flip and repeat searing, then place chicken on the clean plate.

8   Repeat with remaining chicken, then place all chicken back in the skillet and add to the oven. Cook for 5-10 minutes, or until no pink remains in the thickest pieces. Set aside for just a minute.

9   (NOTE: if you plan to have leftovers, only use as much spinach as you're going to serve that night). Heat a separate large skillet or pot to medium heat and add half of your spinach and a splash of water. Stir until starting to wilt, then add in more spinach until all is semi wilted (there should still be some crispiness to the leaves). Add pinches of salt and pepper.

10 Serve chicken on top of spinach with any preferred garnish. Reheat chicken in the oven at 400° F until warmed through, or in the air fryer 3-5 minutes. Leftover chicken will keep in the fridge up to 4 days or frozen 3 months. I don't suggest keeping leftover spinach. Leftover dressing will keep in the fridge one week. Do not freeze.

*Instant Pot
or slow cooker*

BBQ CHICKEN THIGHS

MAKES 3-4 SERVINGS

A woman named Ella May Williams helped raise me, and she is still one of the great loves of my life. My mom did most of the cooking, but Ella had a few signature dishes, including her low-and-slow BBQ chicken thighs. I'm offering y'all set-it-and-forget-it instructions with the Instant Pot and slow cooker, but the result is (almost) the same. Fall-apart tender, juicy chicken that will have you counting the hours until you're home for leftovers. Thank you for teaching me so much about love and faith, my Ella.

BBQ SAUCE (makes a little less than 1 cup):

¼ cup maple syrup

¼ cup ketchup

2 tablespoons vinegar

4 teaspoons tamari or soy sauce

1 tablespoon molasses, optional

2 tablespoons dijon

¼ teaspoon chili powder

¼ teaspoon paprika

¼ teaspoon garlic powder

Pinch salt

Pinch pepper

CHICKEN THIGHS:

1 tablespoon butter

1 tablespoon avocado oil

1 ½ pounds boneless, skinless chicken thighs

Pinch salt

Pinch pepper

TIP: This recipe freezes particularly well; double and freeze in individual portions for ready-to-reheat protein that everyone will love!

TIP: You can sub chicken breasts or tenders for thighs, but they won't be as juicy/ might dry out.

INSTANT POT OR SLOW COOKER BBQ CHICKEN THIGHS
(continued)

(continued from previous page)

1   Make BBQ Sauce by whisking all ingredients together until combined. Set aside.

INSTANT POT:

2   Add thighs to Instant Pot and toss with BBQ sauce. Cover and set to 'sealing'. Set Instant Pot to 'manual' for 13 minutes. Cook, then allow to come to pressure naturally (do not release manually).

3   Press 'cancel' and set Instant Pot back to 'saute'. Allow the sauce to reduce, stirring frequently, 5-7 minutes, until thickened noticeably.

SLOW COOKER:

2   Add thighs to slow cooker and top with BBQ sauce. Cover and cook on low for 3 hours, then uncover and cook another hour, until chicken is tender but not falling apart. Cooking uncovered helps sauce reduce.

Chicken will keep in the fridge up to 4 days. Chicken will freeze up to 3 months. Reheat chicken in the microwave or in the oven at 350° F until warmed through.

GREEK LEMONY CHICKEN & RICE SOUP

Chicken soup is absolutely good for the soul...and actually, science agrees! When stress compromises your immune system, this recipe is a great way to provide gut-healing nutrition, delivered in a creamy, bright broth. Feel free to sub another grain for rice and just watch the cook time.

MAKES 6 SERVINGS

2 tablespoons avocado oil

1 ½ pounds boneless chicken breasts or thighs, diced into ¾" pieces

2 medium carrots, peeled and diced into ½" pieces

½ small yellow onion, diced into ¼" pieces

1 medium shallot, diced into ¼" pieces

3 cloves garlic, minced

½ teaspoon salt, plus more to taste

½ teaspoon black pepper

1 ½ teaspoons dried oregano

32 ounces low-sodium chicken broth

4 lemons

1 cup uncooked long-grain brown rice, rinsed under cold water for 20 seconds (long-grain will be brown Basmati or brown Jasmine)

1 cup canned, full-fat coconut milk

2 large egg yolks

TIP: Save leftover coconut milk for smoothies and other recipes. Save leftover egg whites and mix with another egg to make an omelet the next morning.

TIP: Freeze leftover onion for future recipes.

1 Grab a heat-proof bowl and set it near the stove.

2 Heat a stock pot to medium-high and add oil. When oil moves quickly around the pan and a splash of water sizzles, add chicken. Sear until golden brown on the bottom, then turn and repeat, 8-10 minutes total (it's OK if you don't turn each piece, we just want some browning overall). Scrape chicken into bowl.

3 Add a splash of broth, scraping up browned bits, then add diced carrots, onion and shallots. Saute until onion and shallots are translucent, 4-6 minutes. Add garlic, salt, pepper and oregano and stir constantly for 30 seconds.

4 Add broth and 2 cups water. Zest one of your lemons and add zest, then juice all lemons and add all of the juice. Stir in brown rice and seared chicken. Bring soup to a simmer, partially cover and simmer 25 minutes, or until rice is tender.

5 In a bowl, whisk together coconut milk and egg yolks, then slowly pour into soup, stirring constantly. Simmer another 5 minutes. Taste for more seasoning. Enjoy immediately!

6 Note that soup will continue to thicken, so you might need to add more water and season accordingly. Reheat in a saucepan on the stove. Leftover soup will keep in the fridge up to 4 days or frozen 3 months.

RED MEAT ENTRÉES

| OPTION:

SWEET POTATO SHEPHERD'S PIE

I doubt that I need to explain why Shepherd's Pie belongs in a cookbook for hurting hearts, but just in case...it's a hug in a dish! Steaming on the counter after a full day of school and activities, Shepherd's Pie evokes the feeling of being cared for, fortified from the inside out. P.S. You can absolutely make this with white potatoes, which y'all know I love. But I personally prefer the sweet potato iteration!

MAKES 8 SERVINGS

MASHED SWEET POTATOES:

2 pounds sweet potatoes (3 medium), peeled and diced into 1" chunks

2 egg yolks (save whites for an omelet or whisking into oatmeal the next day!)

4 ounces cream cheese (I like Kite Hill for dairy free)

½ cup half and half or canned, full-fat coconut milk

½ cup low-sodium chicken broth

2 tablespoons butter (sub olive oil)

½ teaspoon each salt and pepper

¾ teaspoon paprika

SHEPHERD'S PIE FILLING:

1 small yellow onion, diced into ¼" pieces

2 cloves garlic, minced

1 pound ground beef or turkey (I suggest a mixture of light and dark meat)

1 tablespoon avocado oil

1 cup low-sodium chicken broth

2 tablespoons ketchup

2 teaspoons Worcestershire

¾ teaspoon each salt and pepper

¾ teaspoon paprika

12 ounces frozen mixed veggies

Special Equipment: potato masher

TIP: You should have some half and half/coconut milk leftover. Use it in coffee with some stevia, as the base of a smoothie, or in a soup or stew. Or make the Pumpkin & Chorizo Stuffed Shells on Page 145!

NOTE: Feel free to sub 1 ½ pounds yukon gold or russet potatoes for the Shepherd's Pie if you prefer that to sweet potatoes.

SWEET POTATO SHEPHERD'S PIE

(continued)

(continued from previous page)

1 Add sweet potatoes to a large stock pot and cover with cold water. Bring to a boil and boil 6-8 minutes, or until fork-tender. Drain and add back to the pot.

2 Add egg yolks, cream cheese, milk, ½ cup broth, butter, salt, pepper and paprika.

3 Use potato masher to mash to your desired consistency; I like to leave some small sweet potato chunks. Set aside.

4 Preheat oven to 350° F and grease a 9"×11" baking dish.

5 Heat a large skillet to medium-high heat and add avocado oil. When oil moves quickly around the pan, add ground beef or turkey. Saute, breaking up meat with a firm spatula as you go until cooked through, 8-10 minutes.

6 Turn heat to medium, add ½ cup broth to the pan and use your spatula to scrape up browned bits. Push all the meat to one side. Add diced onion to the empty side and saute, stirring, until softened and translucent, 4-6 minutes.

7 Add minced garlic, ketchup, Worcestershire, salt, pepper and paprika, and stir everything together. Add frozen mixed veggies and remaining ½ cup broth. Cook until no liquid remains. Spread veggie mixture evenly into the dish, then top with mashed sweet potatoes.

8 Bake for 40 minutes, then broil for a few minutes (optional) to achieve a golden brown top, just watch closely. Cool 10 minutes before enjoying.

9 Reheat in the microwave or oven at 350° F with a splash of your remaining broth mixed in. Leftovers will keep tightly sealed in the fridge up to 4 days or frozen 3 months.

Instant Pot
or slow cooker

MOROCCAN LAMB TAGINE WITH COUSCOUS

MAKES 6 SERVINGS

Thinking about my year at the Natural Gourmet Institute immediately fills me with such fond feelings and memories. It was the first time in many years that I had felt like my true self, and accepted as such. The first time I recall having a Moroccan Lamb Tagine was near the end of my culinary program. We'd cooked all day, and we finally sat down as a class to enjoy our feast with a glass. Making this tagine takes me back to that NYC evening, and it reminds me that I still have my culinary family, despite our distance.

3 cloves garlic, minced

2 teaspoons chili powder

1 teaspoon cumin

1 teaspoon ground turmeric

½ teaspoon ground ginger (sub 1" freshly grated)

1 ½ teaspoons salt

½ teaspoon pepper

¼ teaspoon cinnamon

¼ cup ketchup

2 tablespoons avocado oil, divided

1 ½ pounds diced lamb stew meat (sub beef)

1 small yellow onion, diced into ¼" pieces

¾ pound yukon gold potatoes, cleaned and diced into 1" pieces (approximately 2 medium)

2 medium carrots, peeled and diced into 1" pieces

1 cup chopped dried apricots, cranberries or currants (I used a 5 oz bag of dried apricots)

1 ½ cups low-sodium chicken or beef broth

1 cup uncooked couscous

Salt and pepper

1 tablespoon butter (optional)

Optional garnish: pitted olives, roasted and salted almonds, peanuts or cashews, cilantro, green onion, red pepper flakes

NOTE: Orzo or quinoa would be a great sub for couscous, if it's easier to find. Add an extra half cup of water for either, and watch the cook time. Orzo should cook in a similar time to couscous, but quinoa might take a bit longer.

INSTANT POT OR SLOW COOKER MOROCCAN LAMB TAGINE WITH COUSCOUS

(continued)

(continued from previous page)

INSTANT POT:

1 In small bowl, combine garlic, chili powder, cumin, turmeric, ginger, salt, pepper, cinnamon and ketchup. Stir into a paste.

2 Place Instant Pot near the stove and turn on oven exhaust fan. Press "Saute" and add 1 tablespoon avocado oil. When you add a splash of water and it sizzles, you're ready to cook.

3 Add lamb and sear for 4-6 minutes, then flip and repeat another 2-3 minutes. We want caramelized, golden-brown edges, but it's OK if not every single piece of meat hits the pan. Remove meat from the pot, add a splash of water and use a firm spatula to scrape brown bits from the bottom.

4 Add onion and saute 4-5 minutes or until softened and translucent. Add spice mixture and stir constantly for 30 seconds. Press "cancel".

5 Add lamb back to pot, along with the diced potatoes and carrots, dried fruit of choice and 1 ½ cups broth.

6 Secure lid, set to "manual" 25 minutes. After cooking, allow pressure to release naturally. Taste for more seasoning.

SLOW COOKER:

1 In a small bowl, combine garlic, chili powder, turmeric, ginger, salt, pepper, cinnamon and ketchup. Stir into a paste.

2 Heat a stock to medium and add 1 tablespoon avocado oil. When you add a splash of water and it sizzles, you're ready to cook.

3 Add lamb and sear for 4-6 minutes, then flip and repeat another 2-3 minutes. We want caramelized, golden-brown edges! Add meat to slow cooker, add a splash of water and use a firm spatula to scrape brown bits from the bottom.

4 Add onion and saute 3-4 minutes until softened and translucent. Add garlic and your spice mixture and stir constantly for 30 seconds. Press "cancel".

5 Add onion mixture to slow cooker, diced potatoes and carrots, dried fruit of choice and broth.

6 Cook on "low" for 6-8 hours, or until lamb is fork-tender. Taste for more seasoning.

WHILE LAMB IS COOKING WITH EITHER METHOD, MAKE COUSCOUS:

7 Cook Couscous: Add 2 cups water, 1 tablespoon olive oil and pinches of salt and pepper to a medium pot and bring to a boil. Add couscous, stir and cover with a lid.

8 Remove pan from the heat and allow to sit for 10 minutes, then uncover and fluff with a fork. Optional: stir in one tablespoon butter. Set aside.

SERVING AND STORAGE:

9 Serve with couscous and any garnish of choice. Reheat in a saucepan with a splash of water. Leftovers will keep in the fridge up to 4 days or frozen 3 months.

SAUSAGE, PEPPER & KALE SKILLET

This skillet is about as throw-together as it gets on the dinner front, and I am always surprised by how good it tastes. I made this often while testing non-entree parts of the cookbook, and I'll substitute the veggies for whatever I have lying around or use pre-cooked chicken sausage instead of ground. Just make sure to adjust the skillet time as needed for any swaps!

MAKES 6 SERVINGS

1 medium shallot, diced into ¼" pieces

3 cloves garlic, minced

28 ounce can diced tomatoes

1 pound/16 ounces ground pork sausage (breakfast or Italian)

2 bell peppers, (I suggest a mixture of red, yellow and orange)

1 bunch curly or lacinato/dinosaur kale (any kale!), stems removed and into 1 ½" pieces
½ teaspoon each salt and pepper

1 teaspoon paprika and ¼ teaspoon cumin.

3 tablespoons brown sugar

4 ounces goat cheese or feta cheese

Optional: pita bread for serving

1   Heat a large cast-iron or other nonstick skillet to medium heat and add sausage. Cook, stir infrequently, until cooked through with golden-brown edges, 6-8 minutes. Add to a heat-proof bowl.

2   Add a splash of water, scraping up browned bits, then add shallot and peppers. Saute until softened and translucent, 5-7 minutes.

3   Add half of your kale and stir until wilted, then add remaining kale and repeat.

4   Turn heat to low. Push veggies aside enough that you can add garlic to an empty spot, then stir garlic for 30 seconds. Mix everything back together, then add salt and pepper, paprika and cumin.

5   Add diced tomatoes and brown sugar. Gently fold to incorporate, then add cooked sausage back in. I know it's a full skillet, but it will continue to reduce in volume. Simmer mixture for 12-15 minutes, until most of the liquid has evaporated. This is a good time to warm pita bread in the oven, if using.

6   Top with cheese. You can broil for a few minutes to get the cheese golden-brown and bubbling, if you like! Serve with pita, if using. Reheat in the microwave or in a saucepan with a splash of water. Leftovers will keep tightly sealed in the fridge up to 4 days or frozen 2 months.

Adrenaline is another neurotransmitter and hormone that is released during stress, which we experience in particular right after a breakup or divorce. Balancing blood sugar may help mitigate the jittery feelings associated with increased adrenaline. Look for a trifecta of fat, fiber and protein in meals and snacks like this, and reduce sugar consumption overall.

GREEN ONION PESTO, HAM & CHEESE MUFFIN MELTS

Part of me feels odd including this recipe, because most of us know how to make an English Muffin into a sandwich. And yet, the Green Onion Pesto elevates these melts from average to something that your family will look forward to on particularly chaotic evenings. This is also a great make-ahead-and-freeze option that provides single-servings more easily than soups and casseroles. So, here you go, and I hope you love them in all of their simplicity!

MAKES APPROXIMATELY 6 SERVINGS; 2 MUFFINS PER SERVING

PESTO:

1 bunch green onions (approximately 4 ounces), rinsed and roughly chopped

2 cloves garlic, roughly chopped

½ cup roasted and salted pistachios

¼ teaspoon onion powder

¼ teaspoon pepper

tiny pinch of salt

Juice of 1 lemon

⅔ cup olive oil

MELT:

12 English muffins

14 ounces nitrate-free deli ham of choice (I use Applegate Farms)

8 ounces provolone, swiss or white cheddar (can grab slices if you prefer to grating)

TIP: Serve any leftover pesto as a sandwich spread or as a dip for roasted veggies.

1   Make Green Onion Pesto: combine all ingredients in a food processor and pulse until it creates your preferred pesto consistency. Caveat: your eyes may water a bit from the onion! Refrigerate and make sure to cover this one; the smell is delicious but strong!

2   NOTE: if you plan to have leftovers, only bake as many as you're going to eat that night. Keep components separate (unless freezing; see notes below).

3   Preheat oven to 425° F. Make sure oven racks are situated in the middle of the oven. Slice muffins in half.

4   Line 2 baking sheets with nonstick parchment paper and add muffins. Spread a generous amount of pesto on the muffin bottoms, then evenly distribute ham and grated cheese on top.

5   Roast English muffins until provolone is melted and edges are crispy, 10-12 minutes (you can swap the baking sheets halfway, if your oven doesn't cook evenly).

6   Spread more pesto on the other halves before sealing and serving immediately.

7   Store leftover components separately in a tightly sealed container up to 3 days. If you want to freeze these English muffins, assemble them without pesto and freeze before baking. Then place in the fridge the night before you want to bake them. Freeze pesto separately, thaw and spread on muffins before baking. Follow instructions above.

OPTION: 🌿

HIDDEN ZUCCHINI LASAGNA HELPER

I added this recipe near the end of book creation, when I polled my community for their comfort-food faves. Lasagna was a top contender, but it can be quite time consuming. So I decided instead to make a healthier and veggie-ful version of the lasagna flavored Hamburger Helper! This is a great option for families with varying tastebuds, and kiddos won't know that every mouthful contains shredded zucchini.

MAKES 8 SERVINGS

8 ounces elbow noodles

Olive oil or oil spray

1 pound ground beef

½ yellow onion, diced into ¼" pieces

1 medium zucchini, peeled and grated on a box grater (approximately 1 ½ packed cups)

4 cloves garlic, minced

½ teaspoon salt

¼ teaspoon pepper

¼ teaspoon onion powder

1 teaspoon dried oregano

½ teaspoon dried basil

2 tablespoons ketchup

1 tablespoon coconut sugar or light brown sugar

1 cup low-sodium chicken broth

25 ounces tomato-basil marinara sauce

1 cup grated mild cheddar cheese (approximately 4 ounces)

1 cup grated mozzarella cheese (approximately 4 ounces)

½ cup grated parmesan, or to taste

TIP: Always salt pasta water well. I use 2 teaspoons for every 8 cups water.

TIP: Use extra broth in the following recipes: 5-Ingredient Miso Drop Soup, Spinach & Fontina Orzo, Bacon Jalapeño Creamed Corn, Sweet Potato Shepherd's Pie, Pumpkin & Chorizo Stuffed Shells.

1 Cook noodles al dente according to package directions. Toss or spray with oil to prevent sticking and set aside.

2 Heat a stock or soup pot to medium and add beef. Cook, breaking up as you go, until no pink remains and meat has golden-brown edges. Scrape into a heat-proof bowl.

3 Add onion and grated zucchini and cook, stirring frequently, until zucchini has significantly reduced in size and looks 'dry', 8-10 minutes.

4 Turn to medium-low. Add a splash of water, garlic, salt, pepper, onion powder, oregano, basil, ketchup and coconut sugar. Stir constantly for one minute, then add cooked beef, broth and marinara. Stir carefully to incorporate, then bring to a simmer.

5 Simmer for 6-8 minutes, stirring almost constantly (it will splash if you don't stir), until sauce has thickened. Add all three cheeses and stir until melted. Add cooked noodles and fold into sauce, then serve immediately with more parmesan to taste.

6 Leftovers will keep tightly sealed in the fridge up to 4 days or frozen 2 months. Reheat in a saucepan with a splash of water.

Instant Pot or slow cooker
RIBS

When you want some juicy, tender ribs but don't feel like braving the outdoors and cleaning a grill, grab your Instant Pot or slow cooker! I actually surprised myself with how well these cooking methods work on some Baby Backs. I love to serve them with my Smoky Roasted Potatoes and some fresh greens tossed with equal parts olive oil and aged balsamic vinegar.

MAKES 6-8 SERVINGS

BBQ Sauce from BBQ Chicken Thighs (page 123; sub 1 cup store-bought BBQ sauce. Double recipe or use 2 cups sauce if making slow cooker version)

2 tablespoons butter

2 tablespoons brown sugar

1 teaspoon chili powder

1 teaspoon paprika

1 teaspoon onion powder

½ teaspoon garlic powder

¼ teaspoon cumin

½ teaspoon salt

½ teaspoon pepper

3 pounds Baby back ribs (I prefer these to spare ribs, as they're usually more tender)

Special equipment: trivet for the Instant Pot

1 Whisk melted butter into BBQ sauce.

2 In a small bowl, combine brown sugar, chili powder, paprika, onion powder, garlic powder, cumin, salt and pepper.

3 Rinse ribs and pat very dry. If you see the silver-skin or membrane on the back, carefully run sharp knife underneath; you should be able to pull it right off.

4 Coat ribs with the dry rub/rib seasoning you prepared.

(continued on next page)

INSTANT POT OR SLOW COOKER RIBS
(continued)

(continued from previous page)

INSTANT POT:

5 Whisk together one cup water and 2 tablespoons of your prepared BBQ sauce. Pour this into the Instant Pot, then add your trivet. Place ribs on trivet, curving them to hug the side of the Instant Pot.

6 Seal, press "Manual", then set to 1) 28 minutes if you want them on the bone with a little 'chew' or 2) 35 minutes if you want them fall-of-the-bone (my preference). Once finished cooking, allow to come to pressure for 10 minutes, before carefully manually releasing.

7 While ribs are coming to pressure, make sure your oven rack is in the upper third of the oven. Line a baking sheet with aluminum foil.

8 When ribs come out of the Instant Pot, place them on baking sheet and smother with remaining BBQ sauce. Broil until sauce caramelizes; it should be bubbling and thickening up. Watch this like a hawk to avoid burning.

9 Cool at least 10 minutes. Note that I discard the liquid in the bottom of the pot. I mix with cold water then dump it.

SLOW COOKER:

5 Rinse ribs and pat very dry. If you see the silver-skin or membrane on the back, carefully run sharp knife underneath; you should be able to pull it right off.

6 Coat ribs with the dry rub/rib seasoning you prepared.

7 Add ribs to slow cooker, layering if needed. Add 1 ½ cups sauce on top. Cook on low heat for 7 hours.

8 Line a baking sheet with aluminum foil.

9 When ribs come out of the cooker, place them on baking sheet and smother with remaining BBQ sauce. Broil until sauce caramelizes; it should be bubbling and thickening up. Watch this like a hawk to avoid burning.

STORAGE:

10 Leftover ribs will keep tightly sealed in the fridge up to 4 days. Reheat in the oven at 300° F until just warmed through.

OPTIONS:

PUMPKIN & CHORIZO STUFFED SHELLS

Yes, it's an odd combination, but it just works! I concocted my Pumpkin & Chorizo Stuffed Shells one lonely Asheville evening, because the onset of fall had me craving Autumnal things and warm, hearty meals. I was more than pleasantly surprised by the result, which provides creamy, satiating goodness and just a hint of spice from chorizo. This is a great option for my dairy-free friends. I know that Lelan has made my stuffed shells for her family several times!

MAKES 8 SERVINGS

1 tablespoon avocado oil

1 small yellow onion, diced into ¼" pieces

3 cloves garlic, minced

15 ounce can pumpkin puree

1 ½ cups low-sodium chicken broth (sub vegetable stock for vegan)

1 cup half and half or canned, full-fat coconut milk

1 ¼ teaspoon salt, divided

½ teaspoon pepper, divided

¼ plus ⅛ teaspoon nutmeg

12 ounces jumbo pasta shells, cooked al dente according to package directions (This was 11 minutes for me.)*

9 ounces chorizo (sub spicy Italian sausage or soyrizo for vegan)

15 ounces ricotta (use crumbled firm tofu for dairy-free/vegan)

1 cup grated parmesan or ¼ cup nutritional yeast

Optional garnishes: Greek yogurt or sour cream, diced avocado, green onions, cilantro

*If you need gluten-free and can't find them, you can treat the filling and sauce like a bolognese and add it to any pasta you like.

1　Make pumpkin sauce: Heat a skillet to medium and add 1 tablespoon avocado oil. When oil moves quickly around the pan, add onion. Saute 4-6 minutes until softened and translucent.

2　Add garlic and stir constantly for 30 seconds.

3　Stir in half of your canned pumpkin, 1 cup broth, half and half, ½ teaspoon salt, ¼ teaspoon pepper and ⅛ teaspoon ground nutmeg. Simmer 6-8 minutes, until noticeably thickened. Set aside.

4　Preheat oven to 350° F and grease a 15"×11"×2" baking dish.

5　Heat a skillet to medium heat and add chorizo. Cook, stirring a few times, until you see some golden-brown bits on the bottom of the skillet, 6-8 minutes.

(continued on next page)

PUMPKIN & CHORIZO STUFFED SHELLS
(continued)

(continued from previous page)

6   Add remaining ½ cup broth and scrape brown bits from the bottom. Add pumpkin, ricotta, ½ cup parmesan or 2 tablespoons nutritional yeast, ¾ teaspoon salt, ¼ teaspoon pepper and ¼ teaspoon ground nutmeg. Stir to evenly combine, then remove from the heat.

7   Spread a thin layer pumpkin sauce over the bottom of the baking dish.

8   Fill each shell with 3 tablespoons chorizo mixture, then place open side down in the sauce. I find it easiest to cup the shells in my palm and squeeze gently so they pop open. Repeat until no filling remains. If there is some leftover, just scoop it into the dish nestled around some of the shells. Sometimes I have a handful of shells leftover that I compost!

9   Cover with remaining sauce, then add remaining parmesan or nutritional yeast. Bake for 35 minutes, then broil for several minutes until golden-brown on top, watch closely. Serve with any garnish of choice.

10 Reheat in the microwave or in the oven at 350° F until warmed through. Leftovers will keep in the fridge up to 4 days or frozen 3 months.

SEAFOOD ENTRÉES

———

QUICK TUNA & AIR-FRIED ARTICHOKE SALAD

If you love a Nicoise salad, you will love this (much easier to make) air fryer concoction! This is a recipe that I come back to regularly; it feels special to enjoy, is incredibly satisfying, and has loads of nutrition.

MAKES 4 SERVINGS

- 15 ounces jarred marinated quartered artichoke hearts (I get 2 7.6 ounce jars)
- 5 ounces mixed greens or arugula
- 4 hard boiled eggs, sliced for chopped (reference page 42 for a recipe)
- 4 ounces crumbled blue cheese (sub goat cheese or feta)
- 12 ounces canned or jarred tuna (I buy 3 4 ounce cans. I recommend tuna packed in olive oil for this recipe)

- 8 ounces kalamata olives (pitted or pit in is up to you, just beware!)
- ½ cup dry roasted & salted almonds
- Olive oil to taste
- Aged balsamic to taste
- Flaky sea salt and pepper to taste

TIP: A few tablespoons of finely diced red onion is lovely on this as well, if you're looking to use up any in your fridge.

TIP: How to make aged balsamic from regular balsamic vinegar: add 1 cup balsamic vinegar to a small saucepan and bring to a simmer on the LOWEST setting. Simmer 20-25 minutes, or until liquid is noticeably reduced in size and can coat the back of a spoon. Stir in 1 tablespoon honey or maple syrup and set aside to cool. This will keep for several weeks in the fridge.

1 Add artichokes to a mesh strainer and gently press out excess liquid. Trim any extra woody/thick artichoke ends.

2 Working in 2 batches, add half of your artichokes to the air fryer basket. Cook for 8-10 minutes at 390° F, until artichokes have crispy golden-brown edges. Note that the second round of cooking might take a few minutes less.

3 Assemble salads while artichokes cook. To each bowl (or plate) add a few generous handfuls of mixed greens, ¼ of your sliced or chopped hard boiled egg, ¼ of your blue cheese crumbles, ¼ of your tuna (½ can), shaking off excess oil, olives and almonds.

4 Cool artichokes for one minute after cooking, then distribute between each bowl. Drizzle salads with olive oil and aged balsamic, then sprinkle with flaky sea salt and pepper. Enjoy immediately!

5 This recipe is not made for leftovers, but you can certainly air fry one serving of artichokes at a time if you're cooking for one throughout the week.

20-MINUTE SHRIMP FRIED RICE

This is my go-to meal when I have leftover cooked rice, but I've certainly used store-bought instant rice before! With very little prep (and cleanup), you can have a meal that satisfies your craving for Asian takeout. Shrimp is a high-protein source of vitamins and minerals, so I love to keep a bag in the freezer at all times. That said, you can certainly swap your favorite protein.

MAKES 6 SERVINGS

1 pound uncooked shrimp, peeled and deveined with tails off

3 large eggs

Bunch green onions

2 tablespoons avocado oil

Pinches salt and pepper

2 cloves garlic, minced

3 cups cooked white or brown rice (reference recipe pages)

12 ounces frozen mixed vegetables

3 tablespoons low-sodium tamari or soy sauce

1 tablespoon toasted sesame oil, plus more to taste

1 tablespoon Sriracha, plus more to taste

Optional: sesame seeds for garnish

1 Pat shrimp very dry with paper towels.

2 Whisk eggs in a bowl.

3 Trim the top and base off of green onions. Slice two of them into ¼" rounds. Dice the rest into 1" pieces.

4 Turn on exhaust fan and grab a heat-proof plate or bowl to keep nearby. Heat a large skillet to medium and add avocado oil. When oil moves quickly around the pan, add shrimp in an even layer. Sprinkle with pinches of salt and pepper and sear until golden-brown on the bottom and you can easily flip, 3-4 minutes. Flip, sprinkle other side with salt and pepper and sear another 1-2 minutes, until completely opaque in the middle. Add to bowl/plate.

5 Turn heat down to medium-low. Add a splash of water and garlic to the pan and stir constantly for 30 seconds.

6 Add cooked rice, frozen mixed veggies, chopped green onions, tamari, toasted sesame oil and Sriracha. Stir and cook until veggies are warmed through, then push mixture to the side so half of your skillet is empty.

7 Add a splash of water, then eggs. Stir until eggs scramble, then break them up with a spatula and fold into the rest of the mixture.

8 Add shrimp back to the pan and carefully incorporate, then serve immediately with the green onion rounds, sesame seeds and Sriracha, if using. Add more tamari, sesame oil and Sriracha to taste.

9 Reheat in a saucepan with a splash of water. Leftovers will keep in the fridge up to 2 days. I do not recommend freezing, if you incorporate the shrimp. If you cook this without shrimp or with chicken or tofu, you can freeze up to 2 months.

This recipe is a throwback to my early holistic chef days, when I often used the trifecta of soaked raw cashews, nutritional yeast and miso paste to form a dairy-free base for traditional recipes. I don't use it as much now for multiple reasons: I have a different perspective on dairy, there are more delicious alternatives available, and these ingredients are both expensive and specialty. But every now and again, I like to hearken back to these from-scratch dairy-free recipes. And this one takes me back even further to my childhood in Baltimore, where crabs and Old Bay Seasoning are a way of life. I am so thrilled with how this turned out, and I hope some of my OGs...and new friends...love it too!

DAIRY-FREE CHESAPEAKE CRAB DIP

MAKES 6-8 SERVINGS

¾ cup raw cashews

3 tablespoons mayonnaise

3 tablespoons nutritional yeast

1 teaspoon mild, white miso paste

1 tablespoon avocado oil

3 cloves garlic, minced

1 medium shallot, diced into ¼" pieces

1 ¼ teaspoons Old Bay Seasoning

12 ounces canned white lump crab meat (I buy 2 6-ounce cans)*

*You can make this vegan by subbing 1 15-ounce can of jackfruit (in brine or without liquid, not syrup). Just trim off any tough ends and remove the seeds (you'll see them). Break the rest up into the consistency of canned crab or tuna. Use in recipe where you use crab.

Optional: 2 teaspoons semi-dried chives

Potato Chips of choice for dipping (I'm using the Trader Joe's Dill Pickle Chips here, but have fun playing with them! Utz makes a "Crab Chip" with Chesapeake Bay seasoning that would be a perfect fit).

TIP: Ideas for leftover nutritional yeast: sprinkle on popcorn, scrambled eggs, use in place of parmesan in pesto, creamy dairy-free pasta sauces or stirred into soups.

TIP: If you don't want to purchase Old Bay, you can make a homemade Cajun Seasoning by whisking together the following:

1 tablespoon paprika

2 teaspoons garlic powder

2 teaspoons onion powder

1½ teaspoons sea salt (feel free to start with 1 teaspoon if you're salt-sensitive)

1 teaspoon black pepper

1 teaspoon dried oregano

1 teaspoon crushed red pepper flakes (use ½ teaspoon if you're heat-sensitive)

1 tablespoon coconut sugar (sub monkfruit sweetener)

DAIRY-FREE CHESAPEAKE CRAB DIP
(continued)

(continued from previous page)

1 Add cashews to a bowl and cover with cold water. Soak for 6-8 hours, then rinse and drain. Alternatively, you can add cashews to a saucepan, cover with water and bring to a boil. Boil 5 minutes, then rinse and drain.

2 Add cashews to a high-powered blender, along with ½ cup water, mayo, nutritional yeast and miso paste. Blend until creamy, scraping down the sides as necessary.

3 Heat a saucepan to medium heat and add avocado oil. When oil moves quickly around the pan, add shallot. Saute, stirring, until softened and translucent, 3-4 minutes. Add garlic and stir constantly for 30 seconds. Turn heat to low and add cashew cream, crab meat, Old Bay and chives, if using. Stir until warmed through, then serve immediately with chips of choice.

4 Leftovers will keep in the fridge up to 2 days (4 if using jackfruit). Reheat in a saucepan on the stove with a splash of water. Do not freeze.

DAIRY-FREE SHRIMP & SPAGHETTI SQUASH ALFREDO

 OPTION:

Alfredo sauce is equal parts decadent and comforting, but I wanted to offer a dairy-free variation that's as divine as classic recipes. I think this recipe totally fits the bill, by taking advantage of great brands like Kite Hill and Myokos, as well as the magic of nutritional yeast. You can also make this vegan by subbing tofu or tempeh!

MAKES 4-6 SERVINGS

- 3 pound spaghetti squash (approximately)
- ½ teaspoon salt, divided, plus more to taste
- ½ teaspoon pepper, divided, plus more to taste
- 2 tablespoons avocado oil
- 1 pound uncooked shrimp, peeled and deveined with tails off

- 5 cloves garlic, minced
- 8 ounces dairy-free cream cheese (I use Kite Hill or Myokos brands)
- ¼ cup nutritional yeast*
- ¾ cup canned, full-fat coconut milk
- ½ teaspoon onion powder
- Red pepper flakes and/ or herbs for garnish

TIP: You can always sub garlic powder for fresh minced garlic. I would use ¼ teaspoon garlic powder for every medium-sized clove.

*For a dairy version, use dairy cream cheese, heavy cream instead of coconut milk and ½ cup grated parmesan in place of nutritional yeast.

1 Preheat oven to 400° F and line a baking sheet with nonstick parchment paper.

2 Place squash on a plate. Pierce in a few places with a knife, then microwave 4 minutes (this helps make it easier to slice!). Cool 5 minutes, then use a sharp knife to slice off ends, then slice in half horizontally. Use a metal spoon to scoop out seeds.

3 Place squash halves on baking sheet, flesh side up. Roast for 30-35 minutes, until the sides give when pressed (carefully!), then cool while you make the rest of the dish.

(continued on next page)

Stress and grief may lead to acid reflux. Minimize spicy and acidic foods to help ease your heartburn. Mild recipes like this could be a good choice for you.

DAIRY-FREE SHRIMP & SPAGHETTI SQUASH ALFREDO
(continued)

(continued from previous page)

4   Turn on exhaust fan and grab a heat-proof plate or bowl to keep nearby. Heat a large, high-sided skillet or stock pot to medium and add avocado oil. When oil moves quickly around the pan, add shrimp in an even layer. Sprinkle with pinches of salt and pepper and sear until cooked through/completely opaque and you can easily flip, 2-3 minutes. Flip, sprinkle other side with salt and pepper and cook another minute or until fully cooked.

5   Turn heat to medium-low. Add a splash of water and scrape any browned bits from the bottom of the pan, then add garlic and stir constantly for 30 seconds.

6   Stir in cream cheese, nutritional yeast, ½ cup water, coconut milk, onion powder and ¼ teaspoon each salt and pepper, whisking until cream cheese is incorporated through-out. Turn heat to low.

7   Scrape noodles out of spaghetti squash using a fork and add to the skillet, along with shrimp. Toss carefully to coat. Taste for more seasoning and garnish with fresh herbs and red pepper flakes, if using.

8   Reheat in a saucepan with a splash of water. Leftovers will keep up to 2 days in the fridge. Do not freeze.

VEGGIE ENTRÉES

—

 OPTIONS:

TEMPEH SLOPPY JOE BELL PEPPERS

Welcome to the vegetarian section and make yourself a sloppy joe! Tempeh, made from compressed fermented soybeans, is incredibly nutritious and mimics ground meat quite well. I love how this recipe provides vegetables in its 'structure', so you don't need to worry about making a side dish when life feels chaotic.

MAKES 4 SERVINGS

2 tablespoons avocado oil

½ cup ketchup

2 tablespoons brown sugar

2 teaspoons dijon mustard

2 teaspoons Worcestershire sauce

1 teaspoon apple cider vinegar

½ teaspoon chili powder

¼ teaspoon each salt and pepper, plus more to taste

8 ounces tempeh, crumbled

4 red/orange/yellow bell peppers (any mixture), tops sliced out and hollowed out with a paring knife (be careful doing this!)*

Green bell pepper, diced into ¼" pieces

½ yellow onion, diced into ¼" pieces

2 cloves garlic, minced

4 ounces mild cheddar cheese, grated (optional)

Plain Greek yogurt or sour cream for serving (optional)

*You can trim the base to make peppers stand upright. Dice what's left on the bell pepper tops and add to the mixture when you add green bell pepper and onions.

1   Preheat oven to 400° F and grease an 8"×8" baking dish.

2   In a mixing bowl, whisk together ketchup, brown sugar, dijon, Worcestershire sauce, apple cider vinegar, chili powder, salt and pepper.

3   Heat a large skillet to medium and add oil. When oil moves quickly around the pan, add crumbled tempeh, bell pepper and onion. Cook, stirring every few minutes, until veggies are softened and everything has golden-brown edges, 8-10 minutes. Add splashes of water as necessary to prevent burning. Add garlic and cook for another 30 seconds, then fold in ketchup mixture. Cook another minute, stirring, then remove from heat. Taste for more seasoning.

4   Fill bell peppers evenly with sloppy joe mixture and bake for 45 minutes. Then, if using cheese, top with cheese and broil until melted, watch closely. Serve immediately with yogurt or sour cream, if using.

5   Reheat in the microwave or in the oven at 350° F until warmed through. Leftovers will keep in the fridge up to 4 days. You can make these without baking and freeze up to 3 months. Place in the fridge the night before cooking, then bake according to directions above, adding a few minutes to compensate for the extra chill!

FIESTA SALAD KITS
with BBQ Ranch

I got really into salad kits this past year. For some reason, assembling a salad feels absolutely unsurmountable when you're grieving or just super busy. Having everything portioned out and ready to go with a quick toss is a game-changer. Especially when they taste like this one! I find these Fiesta Salad kits pretty filling as-is, but you can certainly top them with any protein of choice.

MAKES 4 SERVINGS

18 ounces romaine lettuce, sliced into ½" thick strips

9 ounce bag pre-shredded cabbage or coleslaw mix

½ small red onion, diced into ¼" pieces

4 ounces cotija cheese (sub whatever cheese you prefer; I also prefer grated Pepper Jack)

2 tablespoons semi-dried chives (I find these at Kroger or Walmart)

¾ cup roasted pumpkin seeds (sub sunflower seeds)

Handfuls tortilla chips

2 avocados (I suggest one that is ripe and one that needs a few days)

BBQ RANCH:

½ cup tomato-based BBQ sauce of choice

½ cup plain, full-fat Greek yogurt (you can use one of the single-serving 7 ounce cups as well)

¼ cup mayonnaise

1 tablespoon semi-dried chives

¼ teaspoon chili powder

¼ teaspoon garlic powder

¼ teaspoon pepper

Pinch salt

¼ cup unsweetened milk of choice

1 teaspoon Worcestershire sauce

1 teaspoon apple cider vinegar or white vinegar

TIP: Use leftover BBQ sauce in the Rotisserie Chicken Brunswick Stew and Instant Pot/slow cooker Ribs.

TIP: Leftover red onion can be diced and frozen to use in future cooked recipes.

TIP: Store leftover avocado with the pit in and skin on, in a Tupperware container filled with ice water, in the fridge. You'll have to pat it dry before using, but I find that this helps prevent browning!

1   Grab 4 1-gallon resealable bags. In each, combine ¼ of your romaine (5 loose cups), coleslaw (1 packed cup), diced onion (2 rounded tablespoons), cheese (½ cup) and semi-dried chives (½ tablespoon each). Seal and refrigerate.

2   Make BBQ Ranch by combining all ingredients in a bowl and whisking until creamy. Refrigerate.

3   When you're ready to enjoy a salad, add one gallon bag to your serving bowl, then top with 2-3 tablespoons pumpkin seeds and a handful of tortilla chips, crushing them a bit as you add them. Dice and add half an avocado, drizzle with BBQ Ranch to taste and enjoy immediately!

4   Kits will last up to 5 days in the fridge. Do not freeze.

Monday

SESAME TOFU, EGGPLANT & COCONUT RICE BOWLS

I've been making variations of this recipe for over 6 years, and I still love it. To me, this is the epitome of plant-based comfort food, and I always lean towards it on particularly stressful weeks. If you're unsure about tofu, this is a greater starter recipe, because the magic is in the sauce. Which, by the way, you can totally double and use as a salad dressing or veggie dip or marinade for other proteins.

MAKES 6 SERVINGS

TOFU + EGGPLANT:

6 tablespoons tamari or soy sauce

½ cup unsalted, unsweetened, runny peanut butter (smooth or crunchy; sub almond butter or tahini)

¼ cup avocado oil

2 tablespoons apple cider vinegar

¼ cup maple syrup

2 cloves garlic, minced

2 tablespoons toasted sesame oil

½ teaspoon ground ginger

15-16 ounces extra firm tofu, rinsed, dried and diced into 1" cubes

1 medium eggplant, base and top removed and diced into 1" cubes

COCONUT RICE:

1 ½ cups long-grain rice (such as Jasmine or Basmati)

13.5 ounce can full-fat coconut milk

Pinch of salt

Optional garnish: avocado, chopped roasted cashews or honey roasted peanuts, red pepper flakes, Sriracha, thinly sliced cucumber, kimchi

1 Preheat oven to 400° F and line a baking sheet with nonstick parchment.

2 In a large mixing bowl, whisk together tamari, peanut butter, avocado oil, apple cider vinegar, maple syrup, garlic, toasted sesame oil and ground ginger. Scrape half of your sauce into a jar/dish and refrigerate.

3 Add tofu and eggplant to the mixing bowl and toss to coat. Spread on baking sheet in an even layer, shaking off excess as you go. Bake for 35 minutes, flipping halfway.

4 While tofu and eggplant are baking, make coconut rice. Rinse rice in a mesh strainer for 30 seconds. Drain thoroughly. Add rice and entire can of coconut milk to a medium saucepan and ¾ cup water.

5 Bring to a boil, then immediately turn down to the lowest heat, cover and simmer for 18 minutes.

6 Remove from the heat and cover with a DISH TOWEL. Allow to rest for another 15 minutes, before adding a pinch of salt and fluffing with a fork.

7 Serve tofu/eggplant mixture with coconut rice and any garnish of choice. Reheat in the microwave or in a saucepan with a splash of water. Leftovers will keep in the fridge up to 4 days. You can freeze up to 4 months, but note that tofu has a spongy texture when it thaws (which I don't mind!).

CHARRED GAZPACHO
with Garlic Bread

I could count on my mom's gazpacho every Summer growing up in Baltimore. It took me a few tentative tries to decide if I liked it or not, and now I crave it for a reminder of those balmy screened-in porch evenings. My mom's recipe was inspired by the *Silver Palate Cookbook*, which calls for raw egg yolk. Instead, I blend olive oil into the tomato base to add a silky quality in addition to bright, crisp veggies.

MAKES 6-8 SERVINGS

GAZPACHO:

2 yellow, orange, or red bell peppers, roughly diced into 1" pieces

1 pint grape or cherry tomatoes

½ medium red onion, roughly diced into 1" pieces, layers pulled apart

1 medium zucchini, roughly diced into 1" pieces

1 medium jalapeño, seeds removed and diced into ¼" pieces

2 tablespoons avocado oil

¾ teaspoon salt, divided

¼ teaspoon pepper

15 ounces tomato sauce

¼ cup olive oil

2 ½ tablespoons red wine vinegar

½ teaspoon garlic powder

2 teaspoons white sugar (sub monkfruit)

1 clove garlic, roughly chopped

2 slices multigrain or sourdough bread, roughly broken into 1" pieces

Optional: fresh chopped parsley and grated parmesan for serving

GARLIC BREAD:

1 stick unsalted butter (½ cup, 4 ounces)

4 cloves garlic, minced

Optional: 2 teaspoons semi-dried chives

Pinches salt

Remaining loaf of bread

TIP: Ideas for leftover parsley: blend with EVOO and freeze for when need fresh; mix with butter and garlic for simple herb butter; chop and add to EVOO with red pepper, salt and garlic for dipping with bread; chop add to rice; add to salad greens.

1 Set oven to broil and grease a baking sheet. Add diced bell peppers, tomatoes, onion, zucchini and jalapeño (it's OK if they overlap) and drizzle with avocado oil and ¼ teaspoon each salt and pepper. Broil for 8-10 minutes, or until veggies have some dark brown 'char' on the top. Watch carefully! Set aside to cool.

2 Pour tomato sauce into a large mixing bowl, around 8 quarts. Refill tomato can twice with water, gently swirl and add to the bowl. Whisk in olive oil, vinegar, remaining ½ teaspoon salt, garlic powder and sugar.

(continued on next page)

CHARRED GAZPACHO WITH GARLIC BREAD
(continued)

(continued from previous page)

3   If using a 14-cup food processor, you can do this all in one batch. Otherwise, split into two (one piece of bread per batch, garlic can go in either). Add bread to processor and pulse 3-4 times. Add veggies and garlic and pulse just until broken down into a chunky 'paste'. Fold veggies into tomato sauce mixture. Refrigerate for at least 4 hours and up to overnight before serving. Serve with fresh herbs and parmesan, if using.

4   Preheat oven to 400° F. Slice your loaf of bread.

5   Combine butter and garlic in a microwave-safe bowl. Microwave for 25 seconds, or JUST until you can stir together. Fold in chives, if using.

6   *NOTE: if you want garlic bread leftovers, only bake as much as you need tonight and repeat this step for subsequent nights. Spread a generous amount of garlic butter on bread slices and bake until they reach your desired doneness. Sprinkle with a pinch of salt before serving with gazpacho.

7   Leftover soup will keep tightly sealed in the fridge up to 4 days. I do not recommend freezing.

CARROT GINGER & TURMERIC SOUP

This anti-inflammatory soup is an amazing, delectable way to nourish an aching heart, while pumping your body with nutrition. I always go back for a second bowl, and I love to serve it with homemade croutons: dice up a few pieces of stale bread and grill in a skillet on medium with a layer of olive oil until golden-brown on both sides. Add any seasoning you like!

MAKES 4-6 SERVINGS

- 6-7 medium carrots, peeled and diced into 1" pieces (approximately 1 pound)

- 2 medium russet potatoes, peeled and diced into 1" pieces (approximately 1 ¼ pounds)

- ½ yellow onion, diced to 1" pieces (then separate any layers)

- 4 cloves garlic, whole, leave skin on

- 1 teaspoon salt, plus more to taste

- ¼ teaspoon pepper

- 2 tablespoons avocado oil

- 32 ounces vegetable broth

- 2 teaspoons mild/white miso paste (optional but adds richness and nutrition)

- 1 cup canned, full-fat coconut milk or half and half

- 1 ½" piece fresh ginger, grated

- ½ teaspoon ground turmeric

TIP: Use leftover miso in Chicken Caesar Wrap, 5-Ingredient Miso Drop Soup, Dairy-Free Chesapeake Crab Dip.

When the body has excess stress hormones, the immune system can become compromised, which can lead to increased vulnerability to bugs and illnesses, aka the common phenomenon of a "breakup cold." Immune boosting foods like turmeric in this recipe can help combat potential illness.

CARROT GINGER & TURMERIC SOUP
(continued)

(continued from previous page)

1 Preheat oven to 410° F and grab a baking sheet.

2 In a large mixing bowl, combine carrots, potatoes, onion, garlic cloves, ¼ teaspoon salt, pepper and oil. Toss to coat, then spread evenly over baking sheet. It's OK if there is some overlap.

3 Roast for 30 minutes, or until edges are golden brown and potatoes are tender. Allow to cool 10 minutes.

4 During this time, combine stock, miso, milk, ginger, pinch of pepper and remaining ½ teaspoon salt in a high-powered blender. You can also add to a soup pot if you have an immersion blender.

5 Squeeze garlic cloves out of the skin into the blender/pot, then add remaining roasted veggies.

6 If using a blender: tightly secure the lid and hold a folded dish towel over the top. Start blending on the lowest setting, then slowly work up to medium and blend until soup is creamy. Pour into a soup pot and whisk in ground turmeric (this prevents staining your blender!). Bring to a simmer to warm thoroughly.

7 If using an immersion blender, be patient! It will likely have some small veggie pieces no matter how much you blend, but it will still be delicious. Once blended, bring to a simmer to warm thoroughly.

8 Taste for more seasoning (I add another ¼ teaspoon), then enjoy with any garnish of choice. Reheat in a saucepan with a splash of water. Leftovers will keep in the fridge up to 5 days or frozen 4-6 months.

Grief has multiple physiological effects on the body, including altered taste buds, gas, constipation and diarrhea. This may be because the immune system is impaired, and 70% of our gut is in our immune system. Take note if you have these symptoms and focus on easily digestible recipes like this.

 OPTION:

SWEET POTATO TOMATO SOUP

I cannot imagine a heartache cookbook without some iteration of tomato soup and grilled cheese. My grilled cheese recipe is up in the single-serving section (you can quadruple!), and it pairs perfectly with this creamy, slightly sweet soup that is jam-packed with antioxidants. Sometimes when I can't be bothered with extra work, I go another old school route and serve it with Saltine crackers.

MAKES 6-8 SERVINGS

2 tablespoons olive oil

1 medium sweet potato, peeled and diced into ¾" pieces

½ sweet Vidalia onion, diced into ½" pieces (sub yellow onion)

32 ounces low-sodium veggie stock

4 cloves garlic, roughly chopped

½-1 teaspoon salt (I use 1 teaspoon, but feel free to start with less and add to taste)

½ teaspoon pepper

½ teaspoon paprika

6 ounces tomato paste

1 teaspoon Worcestershire sauce

1 tablespoons maple syrup, honey, coconut sugar or light brown sugar

2 15-ounce cans tomato sauce

¾ cup packed fresh basil, plus more for garnish (¾ ounce)

Optional: grated parmesan for garnish

TIP: If you add cooked noodles to this soup, it tastes like an upleveled Spaghetti-O's!

1 Heat a soup or stock pot to medium heat and add olive oil. When oil moves quickly around the pot, add diced sweet potato and onion. Cook, stirring every minute or so, until onion is softened and sweet potato has some lightly golden edges, 6-8 minutes.

2 Add ⅓ cup veggie stock, garlic, salt, pepper, paprika, tomato paste, Worcestershire sauce and maple syrup. Stir constantly for one minute.

3 Add remaining stock and tomato sauce and bring to a simmer. Simmer 15 minutes, or until sweet potatoes are fork-tender.

4 Add basil to the bottom of a blender*, then carefully pour soup into the blender. Tightly secure the lid and hold a folded dish towel over the top. Start blending on the lowest setting, then slowly work up to medium and blend until soup is creamy.

5 Serve straight from the blender or pour back into the pot. Top with more fresh basil and parmesan, if using.

6 Reheat in a saucepan with a splash of water, as soup thickens in the fridge. Refrigerate up to 4 days or freeze up to 4 months.

*Depending on your blender, you may need to puree in batches. Feel free to add all the basil to the first batch, since you'll be mixing it all together in the end. You can also do this with an immersion blender.

MEDITERRANEAN HUMMUS CASSEROLE

Yes, this is an unusual combo. Yes, I still very much want you to give it a try, especially if you're responsible for feeding multiple mouths. This Hummus Casserole went over successfully with a one-year-old and a three-and-a-half-year-old, as well as both parents. It's essentially like a hummus platter, just in casserole form and all roasty-toasty to bring out extra flavor.

MAKES 8 SERVINGS

16 ounces garlic hummus

12 ounces pita or naan bread, ripped into approximately 3" pieces

2 tablespoons olive oil, plus more for garnish

1 head cauliflower, diced into 1" florets

1 medium zucchini, diced into 1" pieces

12 ounces cherry tomatoes, sliced in half

¾ teaspoon salt

¼ teaspoon pepper

2 teaspoons dried oregano

1 teaspoon dried basil

1 teaspoon onion powder

½ teaspoon cumin

3 tablespoons runny tahini

6 ounces feta cheese

1   Preheat oven to 350° F and grab a 13"×9" baking dish. Spread half of your hummus on the bottom. Top with half of your ripped pita pieces.

2   Heat a soup/stock pot (at least 8 quarts) to medium and add olive oil.

3   When oil moves quickly around the pan, add cauliflower florets. Saute, stirring every minute or so for 8-10 minutes, until florets are somewhat softened with golden-brown edges.

4   Add zucchini and tomatoes and saute another 3-4 minutes until softened.

5   Add spices and tahini and stir for 30 seconds then turn off heat.

6   Add veggies to casserole dish and spread in an even layer. Add remaining pita pieces, then dollop on/spread on remaining hummus (it's not a perfect science!).

7   Bake casserole for 15 minutes, then top with feta and and broil until lightly golden brown, watch closely.

8   Drizzle with more olive oil, if using. Enjoy immediately! Reheat leftovers in the oven at 350° F for 20 minutes or until heated through, noting that the pita/naan will soften. Leftovers will keep in the fridge up to 3 days.

OPTION: 🌱

4-CHEESE BAKED MAC

For many, comfort food equals mac and cheese, and I completely understand why! I knew I wanted a mac recipe here, and I wanted to keep it fairly traditional—dairy-ful and carb-ful—but with a hint of health. This touch of nutrition comes from an entire yellow squash blended right into the sauce, and you won't even know it's there. I also add goat cheese for a delightful, subtle tanginess. If it's a mac kinda night in your home, I hope this one hits the spot.

MAKES 8-10 SERVINGS

12 ounces small noodles of choice (I like elbow, farfalle or cellentani)

1 ¼ teaspoons salt, plus more to taste

1 tablespoon avocado oil, plus more for greasing

1 medium shallot, diced into ¼" pieces (sub ½ sweet Vidalia onion)

1 medium yellow squash, diced into ¾" pieces (approximately 2 ¼ cups*)

½ teaspoon pepper plus more to taste

½ teaspoon garlic powder

1 ½ cups whole milk, canned full-fat coconut milk or half and half

¼ cup/4 tablespoons unsalted butter

⅓ cup all-purpose flour (sub gluten-free all-purpose flour)

4 ounces goat cheese

4 ounces mozzarella, cheese, grated (approx. 1 ½ packed cups)

6 ounces medium or sharp cheddar cheese, grated (approx. 2 packed cups)

¾ cup freshly grated parmesan

TIP: Have leftover squash? Dice and freeze it to throw into smoothies!

1   Start a large pot of water boiling for your noodles. Add ½ teaspoon of salt.

2   While water is coming to boil, heat a large skillet to medium and add 1 tablespoon oil. When oil moves quickly around the pan, add shallot and squash. Saute until veggies are softened with golden-brown edges,

6-8 minutes. Add splashes of water as necessary to prevent burning.

3   Add pasta to boiling water and set a timer to cook al dente according to package directions. This is approximately 1 minute less than the lowest recommended time.

(continued on next page)

184   RECIPES *for an* ACHING HEART

4-CHEESE BAKED MAC
(continued)

(continued from previous page)

4   While pasta is cooking, carefully add sauteed veggies and milk to a blender. Blend until creamy. Rinse skillet but no need to clean; we're reusing.

5   Strain noodles and rinse with cold water and add back to pot. Set aside. Preheat oven to 350° F and grease a 13"×9" baking dish with oil.

6   Heat skillet again to medium-low and add butter. Once butter has melted, add flour, whisking constantly for 2 minutes. Then slowly pour in squash mixture. Stir constantly until creamy (it will be somewhat thick).

7   Add remaining ¾ teaspoon salt, pepper, garlic powder, goat cheese, mozzarella and approximately ¾ of the cheddar. Stir until melted and creamy.

8   Pour cheese mixture over noodles and stir to coat. Taste for more seasoning and add accordingly (I add another ¼ teaspoon). Spread mac into your baking dish. Top with remaining cheddar and parmesan. Bake for 30 minutes. Optional: broil for a few minutes, watching carefully, until golden-brown and crispy.

9   Cool 5 minutes before enjoying. Reheat in the microwave or in a saucepan with a splash of water. Leftovers will keep in the fridge up to 5 days. I do not recommend freezing.

Nachos are another lifelong staple for me when I'm having a 'blah' day. They're quick, essentially foolproof and can handle any combination of toppings you prefer. Of course, I love this sweet-savory variation, and it might offer your tastebuds something new. With that said, the most important thing to note is that plantains make for a more-nutritious nacho base than tortilla chips! Sometimes I'll go the 5-minute route and top my plantain chips with pre-shredded cheddar, broil them up and add salsa + sour cream before devouring.

PLANTAIN NACHOS *with* PINEAPPLE SALSA

MAKES 4 SERVINGS

3 ½ cups fresh pineapple, roughly chopped into 1" pieces (approximately ½ medium pineapple)*

¼ medium red onion diced, roughly chopped into ½" pieces

1 medium red bell pepper, roughly chopped into ½" pieces

2 cloves garlic, roughly chopped

2 limes

1 ½ tablespoons maple syrup

¼ teaspoon plus pinch salt

15 ounce can black beans, drained and rinsed

1 tablespoon avocado oil

¼ teaspoon each black pepper, paprika, cumin, garlic powder and onion powder

½ teaspoon chili powder

4 ounces sharp cheddar cheese, grated

5 ounces plantain chips

Optional additional topping ideas: sour cream or plain Greek yogurt, diced avocado, fresh cilantro, sliced green onions

TIP: Dice and freeze the rest of your red onion. Then throw it in the fridge the night before you want to use it in recipes such as Charred Gazpacho and Garlic Bread.

TIP: Don't have the energy to make my pineapple salsa or prefer something more traditional? Swap for your favorite store-bought brand instead!

*Tips for finding the best pineapple: look for one that has a golden yellow ring on the bottom instead of green and definitely not brown! Make sure the bottom gently gives when you press it; it shouldn't feel hard or mushy. And most importantly, sniff the bottom—it should SMELL like pineapple!

PLANTAIN NACHOS WITH PINEAPPLE SALSA

(continued)

(continued from previous page)

1   Combine pineapple, red onion, bell pepper and garlic in a food processor and pulse until it forms a salsa consistency (exact texture is up to your preference!)

2   Strain mixture through a mesh sieve, pressing with a spatula to get as much juice out as you can. Add mixture to a bowl and stir in 3 tablespoons lime juice, maple syrup and a pinch of salt. Refrigerate.

3   Combine beans, oil, remaining ¼ teaspoon salt, pepper, paprika, cumin, garlic powder, onion powder and chili powder in a saucepan. Bring to low heat and stir, mashing slightly, just until mixture is fragrant, 2-3 minutes.

4   Set oven to broil and spread your plantain chips over a parchment lined baking sheet. Top with beans and cheese and broil until cheese is bubbling and plantain edges are golden brown. Watch carefully so plantains don't burn! Top with salsa and anything else you like. Enjoy immediately!

5   If you want leftovers, keep components separate and assemble each individual serving. To reheat, microwave beans then use broiler as above. Beans will keep in the fridge up to 4 days and salsa up to 1 week. Beans will freeze up to 3 months. I do not suggest freezing salsa.

OPTION:

AVOCADO RICE BOWL

This simple meal totally hit the spot on many chilly, lazy evenings. Buttery rice is a warm hug in a bowl, and the flare of bright Asian flavors may just help pick up your spirits. They did mine :). P.S.—This is my new fool-proof method for cooking long-grain rice!

MAKES 4 SERVINGS

1 cup long-grain rice, such as Jasmine or basmati

1 tablespoon unsalted butter or olive oil

1 tablespoon tamari or soy sauce, plus more to taste

2 teaspoons toasted sesame oil

2 teaspoons olive oil

2 ripe avocados

4-8 large eggs

Salt and pepper to taste

Optional: toasted sesame seeds, Sriracha, lime juice roasted salted cashews or peanuts, kimchi, seaweed snacks to use as scoopers

1   Rinse rice in a mesh sieve for 30 seconds. Add rice to a bowl and cover with water; allow to sit 30 minutes. Rinse another few seconds, then drain fully.

2   Add rice to a medium saucepan and cover with 1 ¾ cups water. Bring to a boil, then reduce to a simmer on the LOWEST setting possible. Cover and simmer 17 minutes, then remove from the heat and allow to sit another 5 minutes. Fluff with a fork, then stir in butter, tamari and toasted sesame oil.

3   To serve (1 serving): Fry 1-2 eggs in olive oil to your desired doneness and sprinkle with salt and pepper. Repeat with eggs for remaining servings.

4   Add half of an avocado to each bowl, chopped. I usually drizzle with a little more tamari. Sprinkle on sesame seeds, if using.

5   Rice will keep tightly sealed in the fridge up to 5 days. Reheat in the microwave or in a saucepan with a splash of water.

Heartache may diminish or eliminate your appetite altogether for a bit, leading to hypoglycemia or low blood sugar. Symptoms of hypoglycemia include shakiness, dizziness, nausea, sweating, confusion and irritability. Talk to your doctor if you might be experiencing hypoglycemia. When you don't have much of an appetite, recipes like this can go down easily.

SIDES

OPTION:

SPINACH & FONTINA ORZO

Basically, orzo and fontina cheese are delectable vehicles for getting spinach into your body. It's the kind of dish that warms you from the inside out, and it goes down easily even if your tummy is in knots. This side was a hit with little ones as well. You can sub another type of pasta; just be sure to cook according to package directions instead of step 1.

MAKES 4 SERVINGS

1 cup uncooked orzo

1 cup low-sodium chicken broth, divided

¼ teaspoon plus pinch salt

¼ teaspoon plus pinch pepper

2 tablespoons olive oil

3 packed cups fresh baby spinach

2 cloves garlic, minced

4 ounces grated fontina cheese (approximately 1 ½ cups. Can sub whatever melty cheese you like; monterey jack works as well)

Optional: lemon wedges for serving

TIP: Pour leftover broth into a mason jar, leaving an inch or two for expansion. Freeze for future use or use in miso soup, shepherd's pie, lasagna helper, chorizo shells, jalapeño creamed corn.

TIP: For fresh baby spinach, 3 cups is approximately 3 ounces or half of a 6-ounce bag. This recipe pairs beautifully with the Tuscan Butter Salmon, where you can also use the other half of the bag.

1   Add orzo, ½ cup broth, 1 cup water and pinches of salt and pepper to a saucepan. Bring to a boil, then reduce to a LOW simmer (very small bubbles) and cover until liquid is completely absorbed, 15-20 minutes.

2   While orzo is cooking, heat a large skillet to medium and add olive oil and spinach. Cook until wilted, then add garlic and stir constantly for 30 seconds. Turn off heat.

3   When orzo is finished cooking, turn heat to low and add orzo to the skillet with spinach, along with remaining ½ cup broth and ¼ teaspoon each salt and pepper. Stir just to combine, then add cheese and remove from the heat. Fold a few times to melt fontina, then serve immediately with lemon wedges, if using.

4   Reheat in a saucepan with a splash of water. Leftovers will keep up to 4 days in the fridge. I do not recommend freezing.

OPTIONS:

CINNAMON BUTTER-NUT ROASTED SQUASH

I make a version of this recipe in many of my cooking classes; sometimes with delicata squash or kabocha squash or sweet potatoes depending on what's available. Crunchy toasted nuts and bright, juicy pomegranates balance out the creamy, mild squash. It's an ideal holiday side dish, but I personally make it year-round. If you can't find pomegranates, dried cranberries or cherries work beautifully as well.

MAKES 6 SERVINGS

1 medium butternut squash (approximately 2 pounds and 7 ½ cups, once peeled and diced)

⅓ cup raw walnuts or pecans

1 tablespoon avocado oil

½ teaspoon salt (feel free to start with ¼ teaspoon and add to taste)

2 tablespoons unsalted butter (sub refined coconut oil)

2 tablespoons honey (sub maple syrup)

½ teaspoon cinnamon

¼ cup pomegranate seeds

TIP: You can omit nuts and pomegranate seeds if you like. It's still delicious!

1 Preheat oven to 410° F. Place pecans on a baking sheet and roast for 6 minutes. Remove from baking sheet and set aside to cool. Reuse baking sheet for squash.

2 Trim top and base off of squash. Peel until it reaches the golden layer (usually 2 swipes over each spot). Holding squash vertically and using a sharp knife, slice in half. If you're having trouble with this, microwave squash for 2 minutes, then slice (careful; it will be hot!).

3 Use a metal spoon to scoop out the seeds, then dice squash into 1" pieces.

4 Add squash to baking sheet and toss with avocado oil and salt. Spread in an even layer and roast for 30 minutes, or until tender with golden-brown edges.

5 When squash has a few minutes left in the oven, combine butter, honey and cinnamon in a microwave-safe dish. Microwave 20 seconds, then stir until it forms a paste. Roughly chop pecans.

6 When squash comes out of the oven, drizzle with butter mixture, gently tossing to coat. Sprinkle with pecans and pomegranate seeds and serve immediately.

7 Reheat in the oven at 300° F until warmed through. Leftovers will keep in the fridge up to 3 days. I do not recommend freezing.

Is it a craving or is it hunger? Cravings may be emotion-based, memory-based or a sign of true hunger. If it is hunger, the desire should go away after you've consumed something nutritious with the fat, fiber protein trifecta. Evaluate how you feel afterwards. Sometimes, we just need the original comfort craving!

AIR FRYER BUFFALO CAULIFLOWER BITES

Jonesing for some classic fried chicken wings? Well, this is definitely not a direct substitute, but it can create a satisfyingly similar experience, and you get tons of fiber in return! My Air Fryer Buffalo Cauliflower turns eating your veggies from a chore into a pleasure. This is an updated recipe from my blog years ago, and it's become a staple in many homes, hopefully yours included soon.

MAKES 4 SERVINGS

- 2 or 4 tablespoons Frank's Red Hot Original (less if you're not a super spicy fan. If using 2 tablespoons, add another tablespoon avocado oil for moisture)
- 2 teaspoons maple syrup
- 1 tablespoon avocado oil
- ½ teaspoon salt
- ¼ teaspoon pepper
- ¼ teaspoon onion powder
- 2 tablespoons nutritional yeast (optional but recommended)
- 1 tablespoon cornstarch or arrowroot starch
- 1 medium head cauliflower, diced into 1 ½" pieces
- Oil Spray

1. Set air fryer to 390° F.

2. Add all ingredients, except cauliflower, to a large mixing bowl and whisk together. Add cauliflower and toss to evenly coat.

3. Lightly spray fry basket with oil. Add half of your cauliflower to the fry basket, shaking off excess sauce (amount will depend on your air fryer model), trying not to overlap.

4. Roast for 10-12 minutes, shaking halfway until golden-brown and crispy around the edges. Repeat with remaining cauliflower, noting that following rounds may take a few minutes less.

5. Reheat in the air fryer at 390° F for 2 minutes. Leftovers will keep in the fridge up to 2 days. Do not freeze.

AVOCADO CAPRESE BOATS

Spring began as I was healing from my most recent heartbreak. I made these boats and would take them outside to the Airbnb porch, when I lived with Megan before moving to Asheville. Scooping up these flavors that herald Summer, basking in the sunshine, was a great small pleasure. Serve them alongside some simply grilled shrimp kebabs and you have a quick, but intentional, meal.

MAKES 4 SERVINGS

6 ounces cherry tomatoes

½ cup packed fresh basil (½ ounce)

8 ounces mini mozzarella balls (bocconcini)

1 tablespoon olive oil

Pinches of salt and pepper

2 medium ripe avocados

⅓ cup Aged balsamic vinegar (or 1 cup regular balsamic plus 1 tablespoon honey or maple syrup, see Tip for how to make your own aged balsamic)

TIP: How to make aged balsamic from regular balsamic vinegar: add 1 cup balsamic vinegar to a small saucepan and bring to a simmer on the LOWEST setting. Simmer 20-25 minutes, or until liquid is noticeably reduced in size and can coat the back of a spoon. Stir in 1 tablespoon honey or maple syrup and set aside to cool. This will keep for several weeks in the fridge.

1   Slice cherry tomatoes and all mini mozzarella balls in half. Slice basil into ¼" thick ribbons.

2   Combine tomatoes, mozzarella and ⅔ of your basil in a mixing bowl. Drizzle with olive oil and pinches of salt and pepper.

3   Slice avocados in half and remove pits. I do this by hitting my knife into the center of each pit, then twisting the avocado and the knife in opposite directions. Scoop the flesh out of each half and roughly chop it. Add chopped avocado to the cherry tomato and mozzarella bowl and toss to coat.

4   Fill each avocado 'shell' with this mixture, then drizzle generously with aged balsamic and remaining basil. Enjoy immediately.

5   You might have some of the filling leftover; it will keep tightly sealed in the fridge up to 2 days. Do not freeze.

SWEET CHILI ROASTED GREEN BEANS

This no-brainer side always tastes good to me, no matter what state I'm in. While I make it most often with green beans, because they almost have this yummy 'noodle' consistency when roasted, the sweet chili mixture is just as fantastic with roasted broccoli, cauliflower, asparagus, snap peas, bell peppers...you get the idea!

MAKES 4-6 SERVINGS

- 16 ounces/1 pound green beans, trimmed
- 1 tablespoon avocado oil
- ¼ teaspoon each salt and pepper
- 2 tablespoon honey
- 2 cloves garlic, minced
- 2 teaspoons low-sodium tamari or soy sauce
- 1 teaspoon red pepper flakes
- Optional: sesame seeds for garnish

1 Preheat oven to 415° F and line a baking sheet with nonstick parchment. Add green beans and toss with avocado oil, salt and pepper. Spread in an even layer and roast for 20 minutes.

2 While roasting, combine honey, garlic, tamari and and red pepper flakes in a small bowl. Microwave for 15 seconds and stir.

3 After 20 minutes, take green beans out of the oven and toss with honey mixture. Roast another 5-10 minutes, until golden-brown and 'sticky' looking. Sprinkle with sesame seeds, if using. Enjoy immediately.

4 I don't recommend reheating these, but I love them chilled as well. Leftovers will keep in the fridge up to 3 days.

STRAWBERRY, CUCUMBER & GOAT CHEESE SALAD

with Balsamic Vinaigrette

There is something so innately hopeful about Spring, whereas in my experience, heartache feels a bit more raw in the Winter. While we can't control the weather, many of us are lucky enough to have access to Spring ingredients year-round. I added this dish so that it can offer a sense of hope, of new beginnings and growth, no matter the season.

MAKES 6 SERVINGS

- ¾ cup olive oil
- ⅓ cup balsamic vinegar
- 1 clove garlic, roughly chopped
- 2 teaspoon dijon mustard
- 2 teaspoons maple syrup
- Pinches salt and pepper
- 2 medium English cucumbers
- Pint strawberries
- ⅓ red onion, diced as small as you can! (sub 1 medium shallot, diced similarly)
- 4 ounces goat cheese

1 Make Balsamic Vinaigrette: Combine in a blender in the order listed: oil, vinegar, garlic, mustard, maple syrup, salt and pepper. Blend until creamy.

2 Peel cucumbers and slice in half horizontally, then use a metal spoon to scoop out the seeds. Slice into ½" thick rounds.

3 Rinse strawberries, pat dry, remove stems and slice in quarters. Combine strawberries and cucumbers in a large mixing bowl, along with red onion.

4 Pour enough balsamic vinaigrette over your cucumber/strawberry/onion mixture to coat. Cover and refrigerate at least 2 hours before serving with goat cheese on top. Leftovers will keep in the fridge up to 3 days. Do not freeze.

WORCESTERSHIRE PARMESAN AIR FRYER BROCCOLI

This broccoli is so addicting, it could really be a 1 serving recipe—and it has been, for me! Just a handful of select ingredients come together to turn a lovely but somewhat plain vegetable into a dish I crave. I actually threw this together one night near the end of cookbook testing, and I loved it so much that I added it to the outline at the 11th hour.

MAKES 2-3 SERVINGS

1 medium head broccoli, diced into 1 ½" florets (approximately 6 cups)*

1 tablespoon Worcestershire Sauce

1 ½ tablespoons olive oil

3 tablespoons grated parmesan, plus more to taste

Pinches salt and pepper

TIP: Steam and cool broccoli leftover stems and throw in green smoothies for added nutrition.

*Do not use pre-chopped broccoli for this. It must be a fresh head that you chop yourself for the best result!

1 Add broccoli florets to your air fryer basket. Set air fryer to 390° F and cook broccoli for 8-11 minutes, or until crispy around the edges and knife-tender.

2 While broccoli is cooking, combine remaining ingredients in a large mixing bowl.

3 When broccoli is finished, add it to the mixing bowl and toss to coat. Enjoy immediately! I do not recommend reheating or freezing.

 OPTION:

ASIAN CAESAR SALAD

Do I say it? I'm going to say it. This is a personal favorite for me. I know that combining Asian flavors with Caesar dressing might raise some eyebrows, but I urge you to set aside judgment. Besides, the inspiration came from a pre-made salad mix at Publix with the same theme, so I can't be the only one who likes it. I usually top mine with some seared and diced chicken, then I chop it finely to combine all the goodies.

MAKES 4-6 SERVINGS

¼ cup toasted sesame oil

⅓ cup runny tahini

¼ cup mayonnaise

Juice of 1 lemon

⅓ cup candied ginger, roughly chopped

1 tablespoon maple syrup

2 cloves garlic, minced

2 teaspoons Worcestershire sauce

¼ teaspoon each salt and pepper

¼ teaspoon onion powder

8 ounces romaine hearts, rinsed and chopped into bite-sized pieces

½ cup roasted sliced almonds

12 ounces no-sugar added packaged mandarin oranges, drained (I use 3 4-ounce containers)

Optional: 8 ounces bamboo shoots or water chestnuts, drained

Suggested: store-bought wonton strips to taste

1 Make dressing: In a blender, combine sesame oil, tahini, mayo, lemon juice, 1 tablespoon candied ginger, maple syrup, garlic, Worcestershire, salt, pepper, onion powder and ¼ cup water. Blend until creamy, then refrigerate at least 30 minutes before serving.

2 Add chopped romaine to a large bowl. Top with almonds, mandarin oranges, remaining candied ginger, bamboo shoots and wonton strips, if using. Toss with dressing to taste and serve immediately. NOTE: if you want to have leftovers, keep components separate and assemble individual servings.

3 Leftover dressing will keep in the fridge up to 1 week.

BACON JALAPEÑO CREAMED CORN

I made this creamed corn during my first month in Asheville. That day, I had cried on and off throughout a 4 hour hike. Tears of joy, tears of sadness, tears of hope. I was exhausted in the best kind of way, and verryyy hungry. I got home, showered, and heated up leftovers of my Bacon Jalapeño Creamed Corn. It was exactly what I needed after a cathartic day.

MAKES 6 SERVINGS

6 ounces bacon (approximately 6 slices)

16 ounces frozen corn

1 cup low-sodium chicken broth, divided

1 medium shallot, diced into ¼" pieces

1 medium jalapeño, seeds removed and diced into ¼" pieces

2 cloves garlic, minced

½ teaspoon Worcestershire sauce

½ teaspoon dijon mustard

½ teaspoon sea salt

¼ teaspoon black pepper

¼ teaspoon paprika

1 tablespoon unsalted butter

¾ cup plain, full-fat Greek yogurt

1. Turn on oven exhaust fan and line a plate with paper towel. Heat a large cast-iron or other nonstick skillet to medium heat. Allow to heat for several minutes, then test a strip of bacon by touching it to the pan. When you hear a sizzle, add bacon strips, trying not to overlap as much as possible.

2. Cook bacon for 10-15 minutes, flipping a few times using tongs, or until it reaches your preferred crispness. You may want to turn the heat down as you go. NOTE that bacon continues to crisp up out of the pan, especially as it dries out). Add bacon to the paper towel-lined plate.

3. Carefully drain most of the grease out of the pan (into a glass or ceramic jar to cool, not in the drain or trash), leaving a thin layer behind, and add ½ cup chicken broth. When broth is simmering, add shallot and jalapeño. Saute, stirring every minute or so for 4-6 minutes, until veggies are softened with golden-brown edges. Add garlic, Worcestershire, dijon, salt, pepper and paprika, stirring constantly.

4. Turn heat to low and add remaining ½ cup broth and frozen corn. Cook for 10-12 minutes, stirring frequently, until corn is warmed through and the mixture has thickened (no runny liquid at the bottom). Remove pan from heat and cool 5 minutes. Stir in butter and yogurt. Crumble bacon on top, then taste for more seasoning and add accordingly before serving. NOTE: if you want to have leftovers, just sprinkle bacon over each serving, as it gets soft in the fridge.

5. Reheat creamed corn in the microwave or in a saucepan with a splash of water. Reheat bacon in the microwave until crispy (20-25 seconds). Leftovers will keep tightly sealed in the fridge up to 5 days. I don't recommend freezing.

SMOKY ROASTED POTATOES

aka Patatas Bravas

This dish is just like something you'd get at your favorite Tapas restaurant. Even if you're eating them standing up at the kitchen counter out of tupperware! I love these with a glass of juicy red wine. You can also brown some cooked andouille sausage and call it a meal.

MAKES 6 SERVINGS

1 small shallot, diced into 1" pieces

1 medium red bell pepper, diced into ½" pieces

3 pounds russet potatoes, peeled and diced into 1" pieces

1 tablespoon plus 2 teaspoons avocado oil

¾ teaspoon salt and pepper

2 cloves garlic, roughly chopped

½-1 teaspoon red pepper flakes (start with ½ and add to taste)

1 teaspoon chili powder

1 teaspoon paprika

¼ teaspoon cumin

2 tablespoons ketchup

1 teaspoon low-sodium tamari

1 teaspoon worcestershire sauce

2 teaspoons red wine vinegar

¼ cup mayonnaise

1 Preheat oven to 415° F and grab two baking sheets, unlined. Make sure oven racks are situated in the middle of the oven.

2 Add shallot and bell pepper to a baking sheet and toss with 2 teaspoons oil and pinches of salt and pepper.

3 Add potatoes to other baking sheet and toss with 1 tablespoon oil and ¼ teaspoon each salt and pepper.

4 Roast peppers and shallots for 15 minutes. Roast potatoes for 45-50 minutes, flipping halfway, until knife-tender with golden-brown edges.

5 While potatoes are finishing roasting, add warm peppers and shallots to a blender or food processor, along with ¼ cup water, garlic cloves, red pepper flakes, chili powder, paprika, cumin, ketchup, tamari, Worcestershire, vinegar, remaining ¼ teaspoon salt. Blend until smooth and creamy. Add mayo and blend until incorporated. Taste for more spice and add accordingly.

6 When potatoes come out of the oven, top each serving with a generous amount of sauce and enjoy immediately. Leftovers don't reheat very well unless you have an air fryer (reheat at 390° F for 4-6 minutes). I do not recommend freezing.

You might find yourself switching from a "sweet tooth" person to craving salty foods. This might be because hypernatremia, or elevated salt levels in the blood, can reduce stress and anxiety. This recipe is a great way to satisfy the increased desire for savory foods.

DESSERTS

—

CINNAMON VANILLA RICE PUDDING

For our last recipe chapter, I wanted to begin with something unequivocally soothing, calming and easy to digest. Truthfully, I've made this Rice Pudding for dinner and eaten leftovers for breakfast quite a few times. This is also a well-received gift for pregant or postpartum mamas. Stir in ⅓ cup raisins or cranberries at the end if you like!

MAKES 6 SERVINGS

1 cup long grain brown rice

1 ½ cups water

Pinch salt

13.5 ounce can full-fat coconut milk

1 ¾ - 2 ½ cups unsweetened almond milk

½ cup maple syrup

2 cinnamon sticks (sub 1 teaspoon cinnamon)

Scant ¼ teaspoon nutmeg

2 large eggs

2 teaspoons vanilla extract

1 Thoroughly rinse rice in a fine-mesh strainer. Add to a large pot (at least 6 quarts), along with water and salt. Bring to a simmer, cover and simmer 15-18 minutes, until most of the water is absorbed.

2 Add coconut milk, 1 ¾ cups almond milk and maple syrup and stir to combine. Add cinnamon sticks and nutmeg, stir and bring to a simmer. Simmer, uncovered, for 30 minutes, stirring every few minutes. Stir constantly in the last 2-3 minutes, then remove from the heat.

3 In a small bowl, crack the eggs and check for shells. Whisk together eggs, vanilla and ¼ cup almond milk. SLOWLY pour this mixture into rice pudding, vigorously whisk constantly as you pour until fully incorporated (if you go too quickly, the eggs will curdle). Since it will continue to thicken, it should be a bit runny at this point, but not watery. If it seems thick, add more almond milk as needed until it drips slowly off the back of a spoon.

4 Serve immediately, or wait 10-15 minutes if you want it to thicken. If needed, reheat just until warmed through. Reheat in a saucepan with splashes of almond milk or water until it reaches desired consistency. You can also enjoy cold, thinning it out with more liquid if you like. Leftovers will keep in the fridge up to 4 days. Do not freeze.

OPTIONS:

CHOCOLATE BLENDER MOUSSE

I have quite literally cried while eating spoonfuls of this Chocolate Blender Mousse. It's full of healthy fats, goes down easily, and provides a hefty dose of chocolate for the soul. As a result, I made a batch of this mousse once per week for months after one breakup, and I even added the recipe to my last cooking class roster. If you serve yours with a side of tears as well, that is completely OK. You're OK.

MAKES 6 SERVINGS

1 cup medjool dates, pitted

¾ cup semi-sweet chocolate chips

¼ cup cocoa powder

1 teaspoon vanilla extract

13.5 ounce can full-fat coconut milk

½ cup unsweetened almond milk

Optional garnishes: fresh or thawed-from-frozen berries, whipped cream, vanilla ice cream, toasted coconut flakes

1 Make sure you have 4-6 heat-proof glasses or ramekins.

2 Add dates, chocolate chips, cocoa powder and vanilla extract in a Vitamix or other high-powered blender but don't blend.

3 Combine coconut milk and almond milk in a medium saucepan and bring to a boil. As soon as mixture is boiling (watch closely so it doesn't bubble over!), carefully add it to the blender. Starting on the lowest setting and making sure that your lid is completely sealed, blend until smooth. You can increase the speed after blending a few seconds.

4 Pour evenly into glasses/ramekins. Refrigerate one hour, then cover with plastic wrap and refrigerate another 8 hours or overnight. Enjoy with any garnish of choice.

5 Leftovers will keep tightly sealed in the fridge up to 5 days. I do not recommend freezing.

OPTION:

Pumpkin Pie is such a nostalgic and warming dish for me, even though we didn't really serve it at Thanksgiving! I started enjoying pumpkin pie as an adult, and I can't imagine embracing Autumn without it. That said, I don't have the energy to make a pastry crust when I'm in heartache or simply busy. This recipe combines the unctuous, spiced goodness of pumpkin pie filling with an easy cobbler filling. I adore it for breakfast as well!

PUMPKIN PIE COBBLER

MAKES 6 SERVINGS

4 ounces cream cheese, softened to room temperature

1 large egg, room temperature

15 ounce can pumpkin puree

2 tablespoons arrowroot starch or cornstarch

1 teaspoon vanilla extract

1 ¼ teaspoons ground cinnamon

¼ teaspoon ground ginger

Scant ¼ teaspoon ground nutmeg

½ cup plus 2 tablespoons white sugar (sub granulated monkfruit sweetener or coconut sugar)

1 cup plus 2 tablespoons all-purpose flour (sub gluten-free AP flour)

1 teaspoon baking powder

¼ teaspoon salt

4 tablespoons unsalted butter, melted and cooled to room temperature (sub refined coconut oil)

¼ unsweetened milk of choice, room temperature

½ cup raw pecans, roughly chopped

1 Preheat oven to 350° F and line an 8"×8" baking dish with nonstick parchment.

2 In a blender, combine cream cheese, egg, pumpkin, starch, vanilla 1 teaspoon cinnamon, ginger, nutmeg and 6 tablespoons sugar. Blend until smooth and pour into baking dish.

3 In a mixing bowl, whisk together remaining ¼ cup sugar, remaining ¼ teaspoon cinnamon, flour, baking powder and salt. Pour in butter and milk and mix to form a wet dough. Fold in pecans. Evenly dollop over pumpkin filling in approximate tablespoons. Bake for 40 minutes, then cool 20 minutes before serving.

4 Reheat in the microwave or in the oven at 300 until warmed through. Leftovers will keep in the fridge up to 4 days. Do not freeze.

Studies show that sugar can act as a pain reliever, because it can release opioids. To balance the cravings, I suggest making sure you're eating nutrient-dense, satiating meals regularly. But I also say enjoy in moderation so it doesn't consume your thoughts.

ICED CASHEW COOKIE & RAISIN BITES

One of my favorite bars is the CLIF Kid ZBAR in Iced Oatmeal Cookie. Oh my yum! These bites are a more natural and nutritious version that you can take on the go. I know that I had a tendency to forget to eat sometimes in the beginning of my grief, and these were a lifesaver.

MAKES 15 BITES

1 packed cup medjool dates, pitted

1 cup plus 2 tablespoons coconut butter, divided, softened to a runny consistency (measure once softened)

1 ½ cups raw cashews

¾ teaspoon ground cinnamon

Pinch salt

½ teaspoon vanilla extract

½ cup raisins

TIP: Enjoy leftover coconut butter on oatmeal, spread onto toast or as a dip for dates or fruit!

TIP: Dip a small melon baller in water and use to scoop out dough, then roll dough between damp hands.

1 Combine dates, 2 tablespoons coconut butter, cashews, cinnamon, salt and vanilla in a food processor. Pulse until it starts to form a sticky, chunky texture (you want it to stick together if you squeeze it). Add raisins and pulse just until incorporated, leaving some larger pieces.

2 Grab a large plate and line with nonstick parchment paper. Roll 'dough' into 1 ½" balls, then add to plate. Freeze 20 minutes.

3 Add remaining cup melted coconut butter to a mixing bowl. Dip bites, turning and removing with a fork. Place back on plate and refrigerate 1 hour before enjoying. Leftovers will keep tightly sealed in the fridge up to 1 week or frozen 2 months.

OPTIONS:

CAMP COOKIES

Camping was an incredibly healing experience for me during my 6 months in Asheville. Time without screens, picking my way through the lush mountainside...there's just no space for anything but the present, and that in itself is a gift. I created these Camp Cookies to have a micro and macro-nutrient dense snack that tasted like absolute heaven after hours uphill. These cookies also freeze beautifully, so I encourage you to double the recipe if you love it the first time.

MAKES 18-19 COOKIES

½ cup walnuts or pecans, chopped

½ cup AP flour or gluten-free AP flour

1 ½ cups rolled oats

½ teaspoon cinnamon

¼ teaspoon salt

¼ teaspoon baking powder

⅛ teaspoon baking soda

1 large egg, room temperature

½ cup unsweetened applesauce, room temperature

¼ cup avocado oil

½ cup white sugar or granulated monkfruit sweetener

¼ packed cup light brown sugar

1 ½ teaspoons vanilla extract

¾ cups semi-sweet chocolate chunks or chips

½ cup unsweetened shredded coconut

1 Preheat oven to 350° F and line a baking sheet with nonstick parchment paper. Add nuts and roast 10-12 minutes, until fragrant and slightly darkened in color. Set aside to cool.

2 In a large mixing bowl, whisk together flour, oats, cinnamon, salt, baking powder and baking soda.

3 In a separate mixing bowl, whisk together egg, applesauce, avocado oil, sugar, brown sugar and vanilla.

4 Roughly chop nuts.

5 Pour wet ingredients into dry and fold until just combined; it's OK if there's still some loose flour. Fold in chocolate chips, coconut and nuts. Allow to sit 5 for minutes.

6 Scoop dough onto parchment-lined baking sheet, approximately 3 tablespoons per cookie. I have to bake in 2 rounds. I suggest using a retractable ice cream scoop and dampening it every few cookies to prevent sticking. Leave at least 2" between each.

7 Bake for 11 minutes; they will still look glossy and a little underdone. Cool 10 minutes on the baking sheet before carefully transferring to a cooling rack. Cool another 20 minutes, or until you can pick one up without it falling apart, before enjoying.

8 Repeat with remaining dough. Once cookies are completely cool, leftovers will keep tightly sealed at room temperature up to 3 days or frozen 4 months.

RASPBERRY & CREAM BARS

I came up with these bars one muggy July day during lockdown. I was in a relationship, but I knew we were both headed for heartache one day. I remember feeling the weight of that sadness. While I couldn't predict or change the future, I could create something decadent-tasting, something that I knew would bring myself and my community joy. I still make these often, rotating jams with the season. Oh, and that heartache did come...but it also passed.

MAKES 9-12 BARS

- ¾ cup all-purpose flour
- 1 ¼ cups rolled oats
- ¼ teaspoon baking soda
- ½ teaspoon baking powder
- ¼ teaspoon salt

- ½ cup plus 2 tablespoons coconut sugar, granulated monkfruit or white sugar, divided
- ¾ teaspoon almond extract

- ½ cup/1 stick unsalted butter or refined coconut oil, melted and cooled to room temperature
- ½ cup plain, full-fat Greek yogurt
- 2 large eggs, room temperature
- ¾ cup raspberry jam

1 Preheat oven to 375° F and line an 8"×8" baking dish with nonstick parchment paper. I use binder clips to hold the sides down.

2 In a large mixing bowl, whisk together flour, oats, baking soda, baking powder and salt.

3 In a smaller bowl, whisk together almond extract, butter and ½ cup sugar.

4 Add wet ingredients to dry and and use clean hands to mix into a crumble consistency. Using dampened fingers to help lessen sticking, press ⅔ of the crumble into your baking dish in an even layer, pressing firmly.

5 Crack eggs into a small bowl and check for shells.

6 In the same bowl you used for wet ingredients, whisk together yogurt, eggs and remaining 2 tablespoons sugar. Spread this mixture over the crumble, then dollop raspberry jam on top. Use a fork or knife to swirl together.

7 Top with remaining crumble, pressing in gently. Bake for 30 minutes, then cool at room temperature for 30 minutes. Refrigerate another hour before slicing and enjoying. They'll still be gooey, but they should roughly hold shape.

8 Leftovers will keep in the fridge up to 5 days or frozen 4 months.

OPTIONS:

EDIBLE COOKIE DOUGH

Pizza check, grilled cheese and tomato soup check, cookie dough, check! When I wrote the precursor to this cookbook, an ebook called Recipes for a Broken Heart, cookie dough was the first dessert I tested. While the original was fantastic, this recipe has evolved and improved over time. The edible cookie dough you're about to make has just enough of the ingredients you'll see in any classic cookie.

MAKES 4 SERVINGS

3 tablespoons unsalted, melted butter (sub vegan butter; I don't recommend coconut oil)

3 tablespoons unsalted, unsweetened, runny almond butter (smooth or crunchy!)

3 ½ tablespoons maple syrup*

½ teaspoon vanilla extract

⅛ teaspoon baking soda (this is for an authentic cookie dough flavor)

⅛ teaspoon salt

3-4 tablespoons coconut flour or ⅓-½ cup blanched almond flour (varies based on the nut butter you use)

3-4 tablespoons semi-sweet chocolate chips, roughly chopped (3 tablespoons will give you a more traditional cookie dough ratio, but I prefer the extra chocolate!)

*You can always substitute agave for maple syrup, which tends to be less expensive.

1   In a mixing bowl (I use the same one I melted butter in), combine butter, almond butter, sugar, vanilla, baking soda and salt. Stir to incorporate.

2   Add coconut or almond flour, starting with the smaller amount. Stir every minute or so for 5 minutes; the consistency will thicken significantly. If it's still runny, add more flour.

3   Fold in chocolate chips and enjoy immediately, or refrigerate for an hour for firm cookie dough. Leftovers will keep in the fridge up to 5 days.

Stress and grief can cause muscular soreness and headache. Enjoying an epsom salt bath with a healthy treat may help relax your muscles and ease you into a restful night.

OPTIONS:

This is another treat that I came up with while the world stood still during the summer of 2020. We were all grieving a collective heartache—we still are—and these Cool Whip Dips seemed manageable even when the uncertainty was manageable. They're meant to be messy and cracked, each as unique as us. If you want to add a boost of fiber and omega-3 healthy fats, sprinkle them with hemp or chia seeds while the chocolate is still warm.

COOL WHIP DIPS

MAKES APPROXIMATELY 12 SERVINGS

1 ¼ cups semi-sweet or dark chocolate chips

¼ cup avocado or coconut oil, plus more for greasing

9 ounce container Cool Whip or So Delicious Coco Whip for dairy-free (make sure it's fully frozen)

Optional: sea salt for garnish

TIP: If you have extra chocolate after coating all of your dollops, pour into cupcake liners and freeze alongside Cool Whip Dips.

1 Make sure there's a place in your freezer where you can place a baking sheet or large plate.

2 Line plate or sheet with nonstick parchment, then grease with a thin layer of oil.

3 Add chocolate chips and oil to a microwave-safe bowl, and microwave in 30 second intervals, stirring in between, until chips look MOSTLY melted. They'll continue to melt as you stir. If you overheat and burn the chocolate, it will seize up.

4 Working quickly: Use a 1 ½" ice cream scoop or use a metal spoon to estimate 2-3 tablespoons whipped topping and scoop onto sheet. I find it helpful to wet the scoop/spoon a few times. Place in freezer to harden, at least 10 minutes.

5 Once chocolate is still melted but cooled mostly to room temperature, grab your sheet from the freezer. WORKING QUICKLY: Add balls to chocolate and coat using a spoon, then lift out of the chocolate with two forks, scraping off excess on the sides. It's a little messy, but I personally don't worry about getting them completely coated! Optional: garnish with sea salt while chocolate is still wet.

6 Place back in freezer for another 15 minutes, or until firm enough to remove from parchment, before enjoying! Place leftovers in tupperware; will keep in the freezer up to 1 week.

Sometimes, when the silence of heartache was deafening, I would take myself to a local coffee shop, just to hear something other than my own thoughts. The coffee shop I'm thinking of makes a lovely coffee cake, and I would nibble at it luxuriously while sipping a latte. These mini coffee cakes can offer the same consolation when you don't want to get out of the house. While I offer a note below for turning them into a standard loaf size, I prefer them in mini form to get a better filling-to-cake ratio!

MINI COFFEE CAKES

MAKES 4 LOAVES, 8 SERVINGS

1 cup all-purpose flour

1 cup oat flour* (sub more AP flour)

1 tablespoon plus ½ teaspoon cinnamon, divided

¼ teaspoon sea salt

½ teaspoon baking soda

2 large eggs, room temperature

1 cup avocado oil, divided

½ cup milk of choice, room temperature

1 teaspoon apple cider vinegar

1 teaspoon vanilla extract

1 cup coconut sugar, divided

Special Equipment: silicone mini loaf molds. If you don't have silicone molds, you will want to thoroughly grease.

TIP: You can absolutely make this into a standard loaf size (8x4x2) pan. Start checking to remove from the oven at 45 minutes, using the same toothpick suggestion as in the instructions.

*Make oat flour by adding 2 cups rolled oats to a food processor or high powered blender and pulsing until it forms a flour consistency. Measure out 1 cup. Freeze remainder for future recipes.

1   Preheat oven to 350° F.

2   Make loaf mixture: In a large mixing bowl, whisk together AP flour, oat flour, ½ teaspoon cinnamon, salt and baking soda.

3   In a separate mixing bowl, first crack eggs and check for shells. Then, whisk together eggs, ½ cup oil, milk, apple cider vinegar, vanilla extract and ½ cup coconut sugar.

4   Add wet ingredients to dry. Stir to fully incorporate.

5   Make filling: In a smaller bowl, whisk together remaining tablespoon cinnamon, remaining ½ cup coconut sugar and remaining ½ cup oil.

6   Fill each mold with a layer of loaf batter, a scant ⅓ cup, spreading in an even layer. Top with a tablespoon filling, using a toothpick to gently swirl it into the batter.

7   Repeat with remaining batter (⅓ cup per loaf) and remaining filling (1 tablespoon per loaf).

8   Bake loaves for 23 minutes, until toothpick comes out with crumbs but not wet-looking (other than the cinnamon filling part). Cool 10 minutes before carefully turning them out of the molds onto a cooling rack. Cool another 30 minutes before enjoying.

9   Leftover cakes will keep tightly sealed at room temperature for 3 days or frozen 3 months.

OPTIONS:

GRAHAM CRACKER SAMMIES

Are we sensing a theme of reverting back to our 10-year-old tastebuds when life throws us curveballs? Yes, I am, and I embrace it! Once again, while this snack may not be the pinnacle of health, it provides sustenance, and it's appealing when little else is. Keep these in the freezer for a treat that will stay with you for a few hours.

MAKES 6 SERVINGS

12 graham cracker sheets (I like the TJ's Old-Fashioned Cinnamon Grahams)

6 tablespoons peanut butter (something that's not too runny)

½ cup semi-sweet chocolate chips

1 tablespoon avocado oil

Optional but recommended: Sea salt flakes

1 Make sure you have space in your freezer for a plate or half-sheet pan. Line pan/plate with nonstick parchment paper and add graham crackers.

2 Spread 1 tablespoon peanut butter on 6 of the crackers, then top each with an empty cracker. Press gently to make sure everything sticks, then place in the freezer for 30 minutes.

3 Combine chocolate chips and avocado oil in a microwave-safe dish or bowl. Microwave on high in 20 second increments, stirring in between, until fully melted. Cool at least 10 minutes.

4 Remove sammies from the fridge. You can either drizzle each sandwich with chocolate, or you can dip half of each in the chocolate (like the picture shown). Sprinkle with salt flakes, if using, then place back on sheet/plate and freeze another 3o minutes before enjoying. Leftovers will keep in the freezer tightly sealed up to 2 weeks.

OPTIONS:

4-INGREDIENT SNICKERS

I remember barely having an appetite when I concocted these 4-Ingredient "Snickers", which turned out to be one of my most popular recipes ever. The snow hadn't even fully melted since I had moved out with my ex 10 days prior, and nothing sounded good. Frankly, including these, but I thought they would be a hit with my readers. One bite to test, however, and I was hooked and hungry! My parents even make these healthy little 'candy' bars today.

MAKES APPROXIMATELY 12-14 BARS

1 ¼ packed cups medjool dates, pitted (approximately 12-13 dates)

1 cup honey roasted peanuts*

1 cup semi-sweet chocolate chips

3 tablespoons avocado oil or refined coconut oil

Optional: sea salt flakes for garnish

*For an Almond Joy version, sub peanuts for raw almonds and add ½ cup coconut flakes to the food processor when you add dates and nuts. After you've pulsed a few times, add ¼ teaspoon almond extract to the mixture and pulse again until it forms the same consistency suggested. Follow the remaining instructions.

1 Combine dates and peanuts in a food processor and pulse until it forms a chunky, sticky crumble. It should hold when you pinch it together.

2 Add mixture to a parchment-lined baking sheet and form into whatever size 'Snickers' you like. I try to make 2"x¾" bar shapes.

3 Combine chocolate chips and oil in a microwave-safe dish. Microwave in 20-second increments, stirring in between, until completely melted.

4 Use a fork to dip each 'Snickers' into chocolate, then shake off excess and add back to baking sheet.

5 Sprinkle with salt flakes, if using, and refrigerate one hour before enjoying. Leftovers will keep tightly sealed in the fridge up to 1 week or frozen 4 months.

Chronic increased cortisol from stress leads to chronic increased blood sugar, which can lead to insulin resistance, which can thereby lead to cravings and increased consumption of sugar. Note your sugar cravings during stress, and focus on treats that contain fiber and healthy fat, like this recipe.

PEANUT BUTTER BANANA BREAD PUDDING

When I asked y'all to contribute some ideas of YOUR go-to emotional comfort foods, banana bread and bread pudding were common responses. So I figured, why not combine them into the best of both worlds! If you can't have peanut butter or want a more traditional banana bread flavor profile, sub PB for melted room temperature butter and scatter some toasted walnut pieces throughout.

MAKES 6-8 SERVINGS

Oil spray or oil for greasing

12 ounces sliced sourdough bread, diced into 1" pieces

13.5 ounce can, full-fat coconut milk

2 large or 3 small very ripe bananas

½ cup maple syrup

⅓ cup unsalted, unsweetened runny peanut butter, plus more for drizzling on top (smooth or crunchy!)

1 teaspoon vanilla extract

2 large eggs

½ teaspoon cinnamon

Pinch salt

TIP: If the coconut milk is separated when you open it—you see a thick layer of cream with liquid underneath—scrape all of it into a blender and blend until smooth. Then use in the recipe. Leftovers will keep in the fridge without separating for up to 1 week.

1 Preheat oven to 350° F and grease an 11"×7" baking dish. Add diced bread.

2 Crack eggs into a small bowl and check for shells. Then, add to blender with all remaining ingredients and puree until smooth. Pour over bread and press until soaked.

3 Bake for 25-35 minutes (will depend on the brand of bread you use), or until bouncy on top when pressed, with golden-brown edges.

4 Drizzle with extra peanut butter, if you like! Serve immediately for a softer consistency, or cool 1 hour for a more sliceable bread pudding. Reheat in the oven at 300° F until warmed through. Leftovers will keep in the fridge up to 4 days. I do not recommend freezing.

CANADIAN BLONDIES

This recipe is in homage to my Canadian roommate, Megan Bruneau! I made a version of this insanely simple and cozy cake several times while we lived in an Airbnb together, with cashew butter. But cashew butter is extra pricy and more difficult to find, plus I prefer the almond butter flavor having now tested it. Maple syrup shines through in such a short ingredient list, and each gooey blondie bite reminds me of my dear Vancouver native, who has gone through so much with me!

MAKES 12 BLONDIES

2 large eggs

1 cup runny unsweetened, unsalted almond butter (I like raw almond butter best for this)

½ cup maple syrup

1 teaspoon vanilla extract

¼ teaspoon sea salt

½ teaspoon baking powder

Optional: ⅓ cup semi-sweet chocolate chips

TIP: Using a plastic knife makes the cleanest cuts, or you can wipe your knife off a few times as you cut. (Of course, save and reuse your plastic knife!)

1 Preheat oven to 350° F and line an 8"×8" baking dish with nonstick parchment paper.

2 Crack eggs into a mixing bowl and check for shells. Combine ingredients and whisk until smooth and creamy.

3 Pour batter into baking dish and spread in an even layer.

4 Bake for 28 minutes. Allow to cool 15 minutes before lifting parchment from the pan. Cool another 20 minutes before slicing. Leftovers keep tightly sealed at room temperature for 3 days or refrigerated 1 week or frozen 3 months.

RESOURCES

Barak, Yoram. "The immune system and happiness." Autoimmunity Reviews 5, no. 8 (2006): 523-527. https://pubmed.ncbi.nlm.nih.gov/17027886/.

Field, Tiffany, et al. "Cortisol decreases and serotonin and dopamine increase following massage therapy." The International Journal of Neuroscience 115, no. 10 (2005): 1397-1413. https://pubmed.ncbi.nlm.nih.gov/16162447/.

Fisher, Helen E, et al. "Reward, addiction, and emotion regulation systems associated with rejection in love." Journal of Neurophysiology 104, no. 1 (2010): 51-60. https://pubmed.ncbi.nlm.nih.gov/20445032/.

McHugh, R Kathryn, and Roger D Weiss. "Alcohol Use Disorder and Depressive Disorders." Alcohol Research: Current Reviews 40, no. 1 (2019): 1-9. https://www.ncbi.nlm.nih.gov/pmc/articles/PMC6799954/.

Smith, Joshua P, and Carrie L Randall. "Anxiety and alcohol use disorders: comorbidity and treatment considerations." Alcohol Research: Current Reviews 34, no. 4 (2012): 414-431. https://www.ncbi.nlm.nih.gov/pmc/articles/PMC3860396/.

Swift, R, and D Davidson. "Alcohol hangover: mechanisms and mediators." Alcohol Health and Research World 22, no. 1 (1998): 54-60. https://www.ncbi.nlm.nih.gov/pmc/articles/PMC6761819/.

Verhallen, Anne M, et al. "Romantic relationship breakup: An experimental model to study effects of stress on depression (-like) symptoms." PLoS ONE 14, no. 5 (2019): e0217320. https://www.ncbi.nlm.nih.gov/pmc/articles/PMC6544239/.

ABOUT THE AUTHOR

Laura Lea is a certified holistic chef, with a decade of experience in the wellness industry living in Nashville, Tennessee. She is the author of two previous cookbooks, *The Laura Lea Balanced Cookbook* and *Simply Laura Lea*, and she has taught cooking classes in-person and virtually to hundreds of students. Recently, Laura Lea has shifted her business to reflect the direction of this third book, *Recipes for an Aching Heart*. She has combined her years of health knowledge with theories of grief, romantic rejection and love addiction to create a revolutionary process for healing from breakups. If you'd like to learn more about Laura Lea's courses, ebooks and private consulting, you can head to her website, llbalanced.com.

ACKNOWLEDGMENTS

To my parents and brothers—Mary Lea, Rick, Jack, Will: Thank you for providing me unwavering, unconditional love and support no matter my season of life. I am thankful every day to be one of our party of 5.

To my closest friends—Adi, Chelsea, Kate, Ashley, May, Allyson, Abby, Megan, Leanne, Jill: Thank you for always treating me like a whole, healthy person with much to offer the world. You reflect back to me who I truly am, when I cannot see it for myself. I have the best chosen family.

To Blue Hills Press—Matthew, Lindsay, Josh: Thank you for giving me another opportunity to share my story and my food with the world. I am deeply aware of how lucky I am that you trust me.

To Lelan: Thank you for sticking by me throughout the ebbs and flows, the new beginnings and the bittersweet endings of this business. I admire you more than you can imagine, and I cannot fathom LL Balanced without you.

To Claire: Thank you for teaching me that I am at the helm of my own ship, and that I do not have to take my life at face value. The tools I learned in your program were the catalyst to not only healing from heartache, but creating a business that can help others do the same.

To my LLB Community: Thank you for your willingness to grow alongside me, to be curious and open to the changes I have implemented over the years. And thank you for the ways in which you have contributed to my healing. I think I have the kindest, wisest community of readers out there.

INDEX

Note: Page numbers in *italics* indicate photos.

MORE GREAT BOOKS *from*
BLUE HILLS PRESS

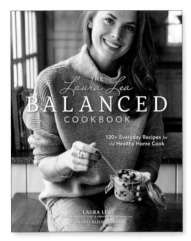

The Laura Lea Balanced Cookbook
$35.00 | 368 Pages

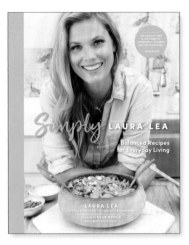

Simply Laura Lea
$35.00 | 368 Pages

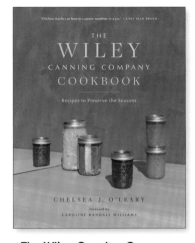

The Wiley Canning Company Cookbook
$35.00 | 248 Pages

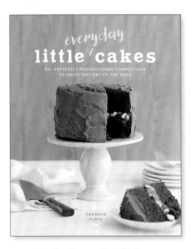

Little Everyday Cakes
$22.95 | 160 Pages

The Hot Chicken Cookbook
$22.95 | 128 Pages

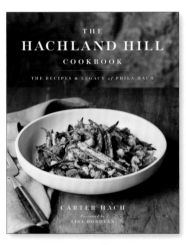

The Hachland Hill Cookbook
$35.00 | 256 Pages

BLUE HILLS
PRESS

Look for these Blue Hills Press titles at your favorite bookstore, specialty retailer, or visit *www.bluehillspress.com*.
For more information about Blue Hills Press, email us at *info@bluehillspress.com*.